May 25, 1991

Jordan,

A wonderful "hero", an excellent "character".
Read carefully and understand.

Joann and Patrick Dunigan

# ROBERT E. LEE

## Great American Generals
# ROBERT E. LEE

## Ian Hogg

GALLERY BOOKS
An imprint of W.H. Smith Publishers Inc.
112 Madison Avenue
New York, New York 10016

Published by Gallery Books
A Division of W H Smith Publishers Inc.
112 Madison Avenue
New York, New York 10016

Produced by
Brompton Books Corp.
15 Sherwood Place
Greenwich, CT 06830

ISBN 0-8317-4074-4

Printed in Hong Kong

10 9 8 7 6 5 4 3 2 1

**Page 1:** *Confederate soldiers on the march pause for a rest.*

**Page 2, top:** *Union and Confederate forces clash on May 12, 1864 during the battle for the "Bloody Angle" at Spotsylvania. This was part of a series of battles in which Generals Lee and Grant faced off during the Wilderness campaign.*

**Page 2, bottom:** *Pickett's Charge at Gettysburg.*

**Page 3:** *Portrait of Robert E. Lee, commander of Confederate forces.*

**This page:** *Lee and his generals. Standing with sword, to Lee's left, is Stonewall Jackson, and seated with boots on, to Lee's right, is Jeb Stuart.*

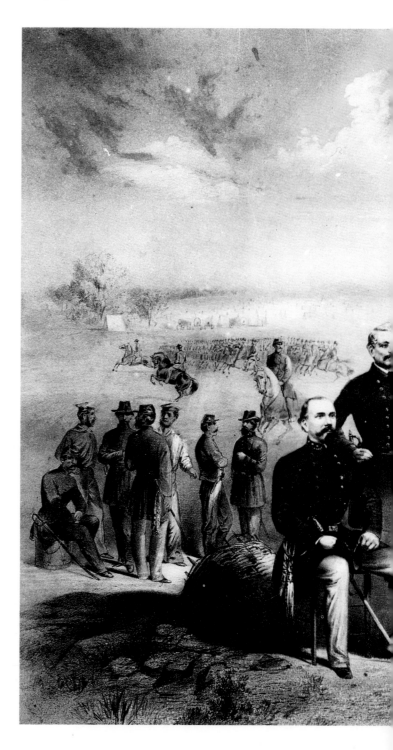

## PICTURE CREDITS

The Bettmann Archive: 4-5, 8, 12(top), 13(both), 17(top), 24, 42, 43, 60-61, 66(left), 72, 73(top), 76(both), 77, 79.
Brompton Photo Library: 2(top), 19(top), 38, 67, 71.
Anne S.K. Brown Military Collection, Brown University: 3, 15(top), 18(top), 21, 30, 31(top), 32, 44, 53(both), 55, 57, 62(bottom), 70(both), 78.
Chicago Historical Society: 1, 23(top right), 28, 34-35, 58-59.
Rutherford B. Hayes Presidential Center: 62(top), 63.
Historical Society of Pennsylvania: 26-27, 33(top).
Kurz & Allison: 75.
Library of Congress: 2(bottom), 6(both), 7(bottom), 9, 12(bottom), 15(bottom), 16, 17(bottom), 18(bottom), 19(bottom), 25(both), 29, 31(bottom), 39(both), 46-47, 48(both), 49, 50, 52, 54, 56, 60(top), 61(top), 64, 68, 73(bottom), 74.
Museum of the Confederacy: 14, 36-37.
National Archives: 7(top), 20(top), 40-41, 45, 65, 69.
Richard Natkiel: 10(bottom), 23(top left, bottom), 66(right).
Peter Newark's Western Americana: 22.
New York Public Library: 51.
Norfolk Southern Corporation: 20(bottom).
U.S. Naval Photograph: 10(top), 11.
V M I Museum: 33(bottom).

## ACKNOWLEDGMENTS

The author and publisher would like to thank the following people
who helped in the preparation of this book: Don Longabucco, who
designed it; Barbara Thrasher, who edited it; Rita Longabucco,
who did the picture research; and Florence Norton, who prepared
the index.

# Contents

# Forging the Sword

Robert Edward Lee was born, not without some difficulty and hazard to his mother Ann Carter Lee, on January 19, 1807. His father, Henry Lee, had achieved fame with Washington's army as "Light-Horse Harry," and it was a fame that rested not only on his dashing cavalry exploits but upon sound strategic and tactical ability. Unfortunately, Light-Horse Harry was impetuous, ambitious, and with a high opinion of his own abilities; he had achieved the rank of lieutenant-colonel but felt that he deserved more, and when the war ended without an advance in rank, he resigned from the army, returned to Virginia, married an heiress – his cousin Matilda Lee – and set about the life of a southern gentleman.

Appointed to the House of Delegates and then the Continental Congress, Henry Lee's future seemed secure. But in the aftermath of the Revolution Britain reduced its tobacco imports, upon which Lee's income was based, and in an endeavour to recoup his fortunes, he began to speculate in land and development. His reach proved greater than his grasp, and he had no talent for business; one project after another fell through, each more expensive than the last, and by 1790, when Matilda died, he had made considerable inroads into the family fortune. It would have been even worse had Matilda and her father not appreciated Harry's lack of business acumen and so tied up the estates that he was unable to dispose of them.

Left with three children, Light-Horse Harry carried on with his speculation, and in 1791 became Governor of Virginia. In 1793 he married once again, this time to Ann Carter, and shortly after this his career appeared to take an upward curve when Washington appointed him major-general to lead a minor force in order to put down the "Whiskey Rebellion." This bloodless affair gave Lee plenty of opportunity for organizing and equipping a military force, but once the campaign was over, so was his military career. Shortly after that his term as Governor expired, but his brief military post has labelled him a Federalist at a time when the political argument between federal and state authority was at its highest; he had made political enemies, and it was an enmity that washed over into commercial life. Although he returned to the General Assembly, and managed, by a narrow margin, to be voted into Congress in 1799, his financial position was steadily declining, and in 1800 he sold the last remaining piece of his first wife's estate that was not in trust for his children. Next came failure to meet a mortgage and the loss of other land, and by 1803 he was besieged by creditors. When Ann Carter Lee was brought to her childbed in 1807, Harry Lee was hiding from his creditors and a sheriff's warrant for debt. When Robert E. Lee was two years old, Harry Lee went into jail for debt for a year; while there he began writing his memoirs, and on his release he continued this, neglecting all else. To make things more difficult, Henry Lee's son by Matilda now reached his majority and, under the terms of Matilda's trust, took possession of the

**Below:** *Henry Lee, known as "Light-Horse Harry" for his cavalry exploits, was Robert E. Lee's father.*

**Below right:** *Ann Hill Carter was Henry Lee's second wife. Her second child was Robert, born on January 19, 1807.*

**Above:** *Stratford, R. E. Lee's birthplace, was built in the 1720s by Thomas Lee.*

**Below:** *Mary Ann Randolph Custis married Robert E. Lee in 1831.*

family home. Ann Carter Lee had had enough, and early in 1811 removed herself and her children to Alexandria, Virginia, a town that she knew well and where she had many friends.

Here Robert Edward grew up, attended school and church, and made his boyhood friends. After the War of 1812, when his half-brother Henry set about restoring Stratford, the Lee home, and his cousin Hill Carter did the same for Shirley, the Carter family home, young Robert became a frequent visitor to both. His father, during this period, went further on his downward path; having been restored to his major-general's rank for the War of 1812, he was unfortunate enough to get involved in a political brawl in Baltimore, that left him permanently disfigured and ill. In 1813 he set off for the Barbados in the hope of restoring his health. After some despairing years he decided to return home, took ship for Savannah, asked to be disembarked at Cumberland Island where the daughter of an old friend lived, and died there on March 25, 1818.

Ann Carter Lee's health was not all that good either, and by the time Robert was 12 years old he was taking charge of the household. His elder brothers had left home, Carter to set up as a lawyer in Washington, and Smith to join the Navy, and of his two sisters Ann was sickly and Mildred – at nine years old – was still the baby of the family. So upon Robert fell the duties of supervising the housekeeping, taking his mother for drives, and waiting upon her when she was unwell. In spite of this he found time to apply himself to his studies at school and to his outdoor pursuits.

But the financial difficulties of the Lee family meant that there would be no college for Robert and thus no degree to ease his way into a profession; the only profession open to him was a military one, and so in 1824 he applied for entry to

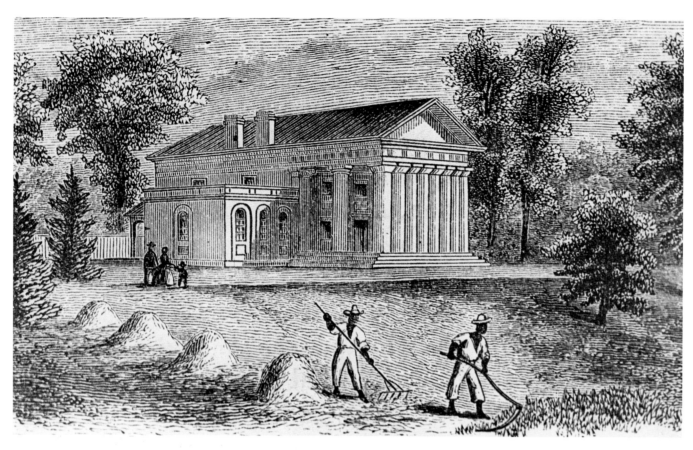

**Above:** *Lee's wife Mary was heiress to Arlington House, Lee's home on the Potomac. Pictured as it appeared in the 1860s, it is now headquarters of the Arlington National Cemetery, which was established on the property in 1864.*

West Point. He was accepted, and entered the U.S. Military Academy in the summer of 1825. Among others of his class was one Jefferson Davis from Mississippi, and a Joseph E Johnston whose father had been a major under Light-Horse Harry.

Since Robert had been raised in rather hard circumstances, the discipline at West Point, which generally irked his companions accustomed to more free and easy ways, gave him no trouble. Without undue exertion he managed to position himself in the top five students of each class, and at the end of his first year was appointed cadet staff sergeant. He went on to achieve a remarkable record – he became the first cadet ever to attend West Point and not receive a single demerit mark. With that, and with graduating as the top cadet, he was commissioned into the Corps of Engineers, the elite of the U.S. Army of the time. Unfortunately, his pleasure at his success was diminished when he returned home to Arlington to find his mother in the last stages of her illness, and he diligently nursed her until she died in July of 1829.

In the fall of that year Robert received orders to report to Cockspur Island, near Savannah, to assist in the construction of Fort Pulaski. While there he corresponded with Mary Custis, a remote cousin he had known for most of his life. The daughter of Martha Washington's grandson, Mary was the heiress to Arlington House and, by all accounts, a somewhat imperious and temperamental young lady. Nonetheless, Robert was a tolerant and good-natured young man

whose attraction to Mary may have been enhanced by the fact that she was the daughter of an extremely rich man, though here Robert was aided by the fact that Mrs. Custis was an old friend of his mother and well-disposed toward him. Despite of the disapproval of Mr. Custis, on June 30, 1831 Robert and Mary were married.

In August Robert reported to Fort Monroe, giving his wife her first taste of life on a military post. Mary did not find it to her liking, and when they went back to Arlington on a Christmas furlough she remained there while Robert reported back for duty. In the spring he wrote asking her to return to his side, which she did, but by this time she was pregnant and gave birth to their first child, George Washington Parke Custis Lee, on September 16, 1832. Within a few months, though, she was back in Arlington "to show the child to his grandparents," and this was to be the pattern of their marriage. Try as Robert might, he could never persuade his wife to put up with post life for more than a few months at a time; she far preferred to remain in the comfort of Arlington House.

Lee's job at Fort Monroe was tedious by any reckoning; in 1819 work had begun building Fort Calhoun on the Rip Raps Shoal, offshore from Fort Monroe, and by 1830, with only the first level of the fort built, it became evident that the island was subsiding. For the next 24 years engineers piled stone on top of the sinking island until it finally stabilized and work could begin on the fort. Lee was but one of many second lieutenants who took his turn at the thankless task of piling stone on stone, but towards the end of 1834 he was rescued by a posting to the Engineer Department in Washington.

The next 12 years were to be spent in routine work, for the U.S. Engineers were responsible for federal civil engineering as well as military works. In 1835 Lee spent the summer surveying the Ohio-Michigan border, and in 1837 he went to St. Louis to stabilize the course of the Mississippi River, spending his winters (when work on the river was impossible) in Arlington. This task occupied him until late 1840, after which he spent a season repairing fortifications in North Carolina before, in April 1841, being sent to design and build new gun batteries at Fort Hamilton, Long Island, and carry out renovation work on three other forts in the vicinity. It is indicative of the position achieved by the Corps of Engineers that part of his task was to determine the number, caliber and positions of new armament for these works, a task which in any other army would have been entrusted only to artillerymen.

Trying to rebuild four forts on the niggardly appropriations allotted was a slow job, and Lee was to spend the next five years at Fort Hamilton. He would probably have spent another five, but in 1846 President Polk sent an expedition under General Zachary Taylor to occupy disputed territory between the Nueces and Rio Grande Rivers. The Mexicans responded by wiping out a scouting party. Congress declared war on Mexico, and General Taylor crossed the border: the Mexican War had begun. On September 21 Captain Robert E. Lee, close to his fortieth birthday, reported to Brig-Gen John E. Wool at San Antonio for his first taste of active service.

Wool's column spent the rest of the year chasing illusory Mexicans who avoided battle, and in January 1847 General Scott requested the presence of Captain Lee on his staff. Scott was preparing an attack on Vera Cruz and Lee's part was, again, the preparation of gun positions, though here he waded ashore from the invasion fleet to select positions on the beaches from which to bombard Vera Cruz. His composure under hostile fire impressed onlookers and enhanced his reputation. After a three-day bombardment, Vera Cruz fell and Scott moved inland to be confronted by a prepared Mexican position at a crucial pass. Lee was sent to reconnoiter the obstacle, and his report not only outlined the physical features but also assessed the various strategic factors involved. Scott acted upon Lee's recommendations, and Lee then led the assaulting troops on a flanking route,

**Left:** *Captain Robert E. Lee at the age of 38, an officer in the Corps of Engineers shortly before the outbreak of the Mexican War.*

**Left:** *American artillery bombarding fortifications at Vera Cruz in the Mexican War. Captain Lee's duties included the selection and preparation of gun positions for the assault on the city.*

**Below:** *Map of events during the Mexican War, including the actions at Vera Cruz and Cerro Gordo, where Lee was cited for his performance and for which he was promoted to the rank of major. He was to advance to brevet colonel before leaving Mexico.*

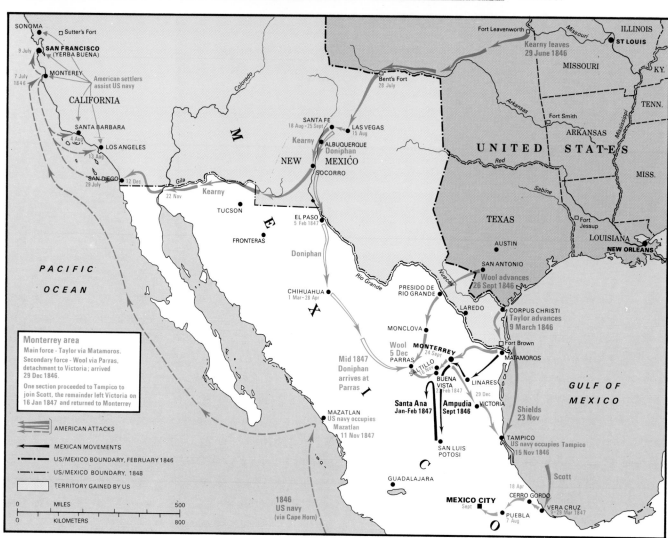

**Left:** *Portrait of Winfield Scott, whose commendation of Lee for his role at Cerro Gordo helped earn Lee a promotion to major.*

selected gun positions, and watched as the Mexican opposition dissolved and ran. Scott gave Lee special mention in his despatches for his conduct at Cerro Gordo, and Lee's promotion to major, a few months later, was backdated to April 18, the day of the battle.

Lee was to gain more commendations for his reconnaissances, guiding activities and supervising the bombardment of Chapultepec, where he sustained a minor wound. He also advanced in rank, first to brevet lieutenant colonel, then to brevet colonel. He remained in Mexico, principally supervising the production of accurate maps, until May of 1848.

Lee's next task took him to Baltimore to supervise the building of Fort Carroll, and then in 1852 he was appointed Superintendent of West Point, where he had frequent contact with his fellow cadet Jefferson Davis, now Secretary of War. After three years at the Academy, Lee received his first

regimental command, being appointed CO of the 2nd Cavalry. This broke his connection with the Corps of Engineers, something he accepted with equanimity since his prospects of further advancement there were slender. His cavalry appointment led him via St. Louis to Camp Cooper, in the Staked Plains of West Texas, where he arrived in April of 1856. Just after a year of regimental routine, Lee was called back to Arlington; his father-in-law had died and he was needed to deal with the estate. Mr. Custis' affairs were in a mess, and Lee took long leave of absence to try and sort them out. For the first time in his life he turned to the running of a plantation, applying military logic and discipline to the problems and, in time, bringing order out of seeming chaos. But on October 17, 1859, after two years away from his regiment, he was suddenly called to the Secretary of War's office. A slave rebellion was fomenting at Harper's Ferry, Virginia (later West Virginia),

**Left:** *The Superintendent's house at West Point, where Lee spent three years (1852-1855) as commandant. At the Military Academy he came to know many of the officers he would later fight beside or against in the Civil War.*

**Below:** *Portrait of Robert E. Lee as superintendent of the U.S. Military Academy.*

and would Colonel Lee kindly go there and take charge of a force which was rapidly being assembled.

Arriving at Harper's Ferry at 10 o'clock that night, Lee found that a band of some 20 white insurrectionists, led by John Brown, had barricaded themselves into the arsenal, taking with them a handful of hostages. Before being driven into the arsenal by the local militia the band had shot and killed two men, had lost two of their number killed and another two captured, and had several badly wounded men on their hands. They were besieged by the local militia and some farmers, though the besiegers showed no inclination to storm the arsenal.

Lee's aide in this affair was Lieutenant J. E. B. Stuart, and in the dawn's pale light Stuart advanced to the arsenal to deliver an ultimatum; surrender or take the consequences. The request being spurned, Stuart gave a signal and jumped aside as a squad of Marines dashed forward, smashed a hole in the door and went in. After a brief struggle, in which Lieut. Green, the Marine leader, beat John Brown unconscious with his sword hilt, the insurrectionists were dragged out. Lee, in his report of the affair, referred to it simply as a riot and played down any suggestions of freeing slaves or incitement to insurrection. But the subsequent trial and hanging of John Brown polarized the abolitionist cause and suddenly made the South realize that there were Northerners who would stop at nothing to impose their point of view. And if these Northerners were prepared to support violent upheaval, killing and pillage, then the South became anti-North; it was as simple as that to the average man in the street.

**Left:** *When Lee was appointed commanding officer of the 2nd U.S. Cavalry in Texas in 1855, his wife Mary Custis Lee remained at Arlington. When her father died, Lee took an extended leave and applied himself to running the Custis plantation.*

**Below:** *Recalled to command a force to end John Brown's insurrection at Harper's Ferry, Lee had Lieutenant J.E.B. Stuart lead a unit of Marines against the federal arsenal in which the rebels had holed up.*

# Jack of all Trades

After the brief but significant engagement at Harper's Ferry, Lee returned to Arlington, but in February 1860 rejoined his regiment in San Antonio. Isolated deep in Texas, the rumblings between North and South were faint indeed, and Lee occupied himself with chasing bandits and drilling his troops. In letters to friends he expressed his dislike of the way events were turning: "I am not pleased with the course of the 'Cotton States' as they term themselves. Secession is nothing but revolution." And he expressed his own position quite clearly: "If the Union is dissolved and the Government disrupted, I shall return to my native state and share the miseries of my people, and save in defense will draw my sword on none." But on December 20, South Carolina seceded, to be followed rapidly by Mississippi, Florida, Alabama, Georgia and Louisiana. Texas followed on February 1 and three days later the seceded states met to form a provisional government. On that same day orders were sent for Lee to hand over command of his regiment and report to Washington.

In Washington Lee was promoted to full colonel and given command of the 1st Cavalry Regiment. A few days later he had an interview with General Scott; there is no doubt that Scott attempted to persuade Lee to accept command of the army which would take the field against the South if war was declared. And, equally, there is no doubt at all that Lee refused.

He returned to Arlington to await events; they were not long in coming. In swift succession, Fort Sumter was fired on and surrendered, Lincoln called for volunteers, and Lee was again offered supreme command. Again he refused, and followed it by his resignation from the U.S. Army. Two days later he was offered command of Virginia's military and naval forces with the rank of major-general; he accepted, stipulating that it be made public that he had resigned from the U.S. Army *before* the Virginian offer had been made to him.

Lee's first task was that of organizing the flood of volunteers who poured in to enlist. On May 10 President Davis, who had appointed himself Commander-in-Chief of the Confederate forces, gave Lee the command of all troops in Virginia, but only for administrative purposes; Lee's function was to train them and ship them into Confederate commands where they would then be led into battle by others. Irksome as this was, he had to admit that he was probably the only man in Virginia capable of organizing these new forces – creating an army of some 40,000 in seven weeks – but it left him dismayed at the prospect of battle when he realized that many of the commanders, political appointees for the most part, were simply incompetent. But his position denied him the power to remove them.

Lee was to spend the next year in organizing defenses, supply lines, regiments of troops, artillery and whatever else Davis felt needed to be done, while battles were fought without his assistance. People began to wonder what Lee had ever done to be acclaimed a great soldier, since he appeared to be doing nothing but command a desk. His first apparent chance at combat came after Manassas, when Union forces pressed against Virginia's western borders and Lee was sent by Davis to coordinate affairs. Lee found three incompetent commanders, who hated each other and refused to act in concert, but since he had no command authority, he was reduced to advising and suggesting

**Right:** *Bombardment of Fort Sumter. After the surrender of Fort Sumter on April 14, 1861, President Lincoln called for volunteers, Lee was offered command of the U.S. Army but resigned and two days later took command of Virginia's military forces.*

courses of action. His suggestions and advice were ignored and at Cheat Mountain a planned attack was bungled, and the Confederate forces had to retire.

Although Lee had done what was required, in preventing the Union forces from entering the Shenandoah Valley, it had to be admitted that West Virginia was lost to the Confederacy; this did not go down well with the Confederate newspapers, and Lee came in for some vicious criticism. Recalled to Richmond, he was next sent down to Charleston, South Carolina, to take over the defenses there in the face of a Federal naval attack. He very quickly organized the available troops, put his engineering skills to work in laying out fortifications, and within weeks had secured Charleston and Savannah, Georgia, to such good effect that, apart from frequent bombardment from Union warships, they were never in danger until near the end of the war.

By the beginning of March 1862 the war had begun to go badly for the Confederacy: Nashville, Tennessee, had fallen and the western armies had been driven back to Corinth, Mississippi; closer to Richmond, Roanoke Island had fallen

**Above:** *Portraits of the two opponents, the Confederate President Jefferson Davis and the U.S. President Abraham Lincoln, at the beginning of the Civil War.*

**Right:** *The inauguration of Jefferson Davis as president of the Confederate States of America at the state capitol in Montgomery, Alabama, on February 18, 1861, two weeks before Lincoln's inauguration as U.S. President.*

to a Union seaborne assault led by General Burnside. Major General George B. McClellan had spent several months organizing, training and equipping a Union army with which he promised to invade the South and settle the war, but only when he was ready, and getting everything adjusted and perfected to his satisfaction was a slow business. The Confederate General Joe Johnston felt secure in falling back from Manassas, Virginia, to lines around Fredericksburg, Virginia from which, he felt, he could move in whatever direction McClellan threatened. But McClellan had a master plan; instead of a direct thrust down from Washington, he moved his army by sea to Fort Monroe on the Virginia Peninsula, landed them, and made ready to move on Richmond from the flank. McClellan's 100,000 troops greatly outnumbered Confederate defenders.

On April 5 McClellan decided to move. He attempted to outflank General John Bankhead Magruder's defenses at Yorktown, just northwest of Fort Monroe, but his battlefield intelligence was poor and he was unaware of the extent of the defenses. McClellan's advance splashed to a halt in unexpected swamps under a fierce bombardment from unsuspected guns. And on the same day the Federal Secretary of War, Stanton, withdrew a quarter of McClellan's troops in order to strengthen the defense of Washington, since a Confederate force under General Thomas J. "Stonewall" Jackson was making its presence felt near Winchester, Virginia, at the head of the Shenandoah Valley. McClellan's enthusiasm for attack soon evaporated and he settled down to organize a formal siege against Yorktown.

To Lee and Davis it was obvious that Richmond was McClellan's eventual goal, and that Yorktown was a digression; sooner or later McClellan might also realize this and get back to his main objective. And so Johnston's force was shifted to the Peninsula and Johnston was given command of all the troops in the Tidewater area as well as those in middle Virginia.

Next, a second Union force, under General McDowell, began moving south from Alexandria, Virginia, aimed at Richmond and a junction with McClellan. Lee managed to get Davis' permission to move some troops, ostensibly to

place a barrier in front of McDowell; in fact, Lee was about to begin putting some military strategy into the Civil War. Hitherto military operations had largely been reactive; wait to see what the other side does, then do something to stop them. Lee was now going to initiate moves which would force the other side to respond in the way he wanted.

Johnston had vanished into the Peninsula and refused to answer any communications from Davis or Lee, confident that he knew better than either how to conduct his campaign. It thus came as a surprise when Johnston suddenly announced he was abandoning Yorktown (thus throwing away the Confederate navy base at Norfolk, Virginia) and retiring toward Richmond. While Lee busied himself in collecting the odds and ends of troops coming out of the Peninsula in advance of Johnston's army, he also took advantage of Johnston's isolation by sending a few suggestions to Stonewall Jackson, leading Jackson to start his campaign in the Shenandoah Valley.

On May 14 there was a momentous conderence in Davis' headquarters in Richmond at which Davis announced that

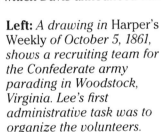

**Left:** *A drawing in* Harper's Weekly *of October 5, 1861, shows a recruiting team for the Confederate army parading in Woodstock, Virginia. Lee's first administrative task was to organize the volunteers.*

**Above:** *Confederate generals Stonewall Jackson, Joseph E. Johnston, and Robert E. Lee. Lee and Jackson were very close and often planned their maneuvers together.*

**Below:** *Charleston, South Carolina, around 1864. Lee engineered the defenses of the city so well that Charleston was never seriously endangered until near the end of the war.*

the business before the meeting was to decide upon the next line of defense after Richmond had been abandoned. For the first time since the war began, Lee lost his temper. Abandon Richmond? "But," Lee cried, "Richmond *must* be defended!"

Lee's obvious passion shook the other members and very rapidly their spirits rose and they began discussing defense rather than retreat. Defenses were hurriedly dug and manned, and on May 17 Lee found that Johnston, instead of standing on the line of the Chickahominy River as might have been expected, had crossed it and was falling back upon Richmond, He was followed, slowly, by McClellan who intended to place Richmond under siege.

McClellan's army was divided by the Chickahominy River, which, due to heavy rain, was flooded and formed a major barrier. Two corps were south of the river and three were to the north, and McClellan was moving his northern force so as to meet McDowell when the latter arrived. But now Lee's strategy took effect; Jackson's activities in the

**Left:** *Major General George B. McClellan commanded Union troops in the unsuccessful drive to take Richmond, the Confederate capital, during the Peninsular Campaign.*

**Below:** *Union General Philip Kearney leads his soldiers at Williamsburg, Virginia, May 5, 1862, against rebel troops who were acting as Johnston's rear guard during his withdrawal from Yorktown.*

Shenandoah Valley routed a Union force, and President Lincoln, concerned about the safety of Washington, halted McDowell at Fredericksburg and sent some of his forces back to help in the Valley. There would be no junction with McClellan.

Johnston now decided to attack the southern half of McClellan's force, and, indeed, the situation was entirely favorable to him. But he delayed until Lee decided to ride out to his headquarters and see what was happening. At the same time McClellan had also decided to attack and what resulted was the Battle of Seven Pines, a confused and fumbled engagement as both sides scrambled through swamps and thickets shooting at each other and occasionally at their companions.

As reports of the confused fighting came in, Johnston, in the hope of salvaging some sort of order from the chaos, rode out to lead his troops to victory just as President Davis, moved by the same curiosity as Lee, arrived to find out what was going on. Johnston never stopped but galloped off; shortly afterwards he ran into a group of Union troops and was severely wounded, being brought back to his headquarters barely able to speak. Since nobody had the slightest idea of what his plans or intentions were, the battle gradually died away as darkness fell. Davis and Lee rode back to Richmond and after some time on the road Davis turned to Lee and gave him command of the army. He would still be Davis' adviser, but after 13 months of behind-the-scenes work for Davis, Lee was at last in a position to take effective command of events. Lee's first move was to issue an order appraising the troops of his appointment,

**Above:** *The Battle of Seven Pines, May 31, 1862. Shortly thereafter Lee replaced Johnston, who was wounded in this battle, as commander of the army.*

**Below:** *Confederate General John Bankhead Magruder was used by Lee in the Seven Days' Campaign to distract Union General McClellan.*

and in so doing he created a new title for the force; it was now the Army of Northern Virginia.

Now came the task of defeating McClellan, and Lee used some psychology. He knew McClellan to be a slow and methodical man, likely to be upset by strange events, and he therefore set General Magruder the task of baffling him. Magruder wheeled and countermarched his army hither and yon, until McClellan was convinced that massive Confederate reinforcements were in front of him. At the same time Lee gave Stonewall Jackson his head in the Valley, to range back and forth surprising Union troops and putting them in so much disarray that there would be no chance of McDowell weakening Washington's defense and sending reinforcements to McClellan. Then Lee moved forces northward and set about breaking the Union force north of the Chickahominy River. To do this he weakened his right flank under Magruder, and just as Lee was about to begin his attack in the north, McClellan began moving against the thin screen which was all Magruder had left to him. Lee studied this, decided McClellan was merely making an exploratory probe, and carried on with his plan of attack, descending upon McClellan's right wing on June 26.

Lee had ordered Jackson to bring his army across from the Shenandoah Valley to assist, but for once Jackson was slow and failed to arrive on time. The Union forces held throughout the first day's battle, but next morning Jackson's and General A. P. Hill's forces were added to the Confederate strength, and the Union troops began to fall back. This turning of his flank led McClellan to begin a hasty general withdrawl of his forces in front of Richmond.

McClellan, to his credit, conducted a masterly retreat – though he never called it that, referring always to a "change of base" – heading south as Lee's forces slashed at his rear and flanks. The whole affair became a simple question of who could move faster, McClellan retreating or Lee pursuing him.

The "Seven Days," as this chain of actions came to be known, was an immense gamble; Lee gambled upon his appraisal of McClellan as easily panicked, and he was right. Magruder continued his histrionics on McClellan's left flank, so that McClellan was never sure of what might come from there, while Lee moved as fast as he could rolling up the right flank. The combination made the Union forces fall back all along their front, and only the relative inexperience of Lee's forces, together with the lack of staff communications due to Johnston's poor organization, allowed McClellan to escape. Fighting a sound rearguard action through Mechanicsville, Cold Harbor, Savage's Station, White Oak Swamp and finally Malvern Hill, McClellan managed to extricate much of his army and concentrate it at Harrison's Landing on the James River, protected there by his artillery and gunboats. By that time the incessant rain had turned all the roads to mud, the men of Lee's army were exhausted with pursuit and fighting, and the Seven Days' campaign petered out.

**Left above:** *Robert E. Lee and his generals. Flanking Lee are Johnston (with goatee) and Jackson.*

**Left:** *Mounted on rail cars, mortars like this were used in the Peninsular Campaign.*

**Below:** *The battle at Malvern Hill, the last of the Seven Days' Campaign, was fought on July 1, 1862, between Union forces under General McClellan and Confederate forces under Generals Lee, Longstreet and Jackson.*

# North to Antietam

With McClellan thoroughly cowed – he could, quite easily, have stormed back up the Peninsula and taken Richmond, such was his superiority in arms and men, but he simply lacked the necessary fire in his belly – Lee now turned his attention northward. Lincoln, despairing of ever getting a fight out of McClellan, had sent for a new general, John Pope, who had acquired a reputation in the West, and had given him command of the troops before Washington, with orders to invade Virginia. Pope made much sound and fury, threatening reprisals upon Confederate civilians, giving his soldiers leave to loot whatever they wanted, and generally upset the accepted notions of war. To Lee he became "the miscreant Pope," and he sent Jackson north to make a reconnaissance. Meanwhile, he made a few feints at McClellan to see whether he would come out of his lair at Harrison's Landing, decided that he would not, discovered that McClellan was sending troops north by water to reinforce Pope, and therefore directed his eyes northward.

Jackson, after harrying Pope with his cavalry, met him head-on at Manassas, the same field that had already been fought over, for the "Second Bull Run." The two sides clashed, Jackson held, and in the nick of time Lee appeared with General James Longstreet and reinforcements. Unfortunately, Lee's command style let him down; he *suggested* to Longstreet that he should attack, striking while the iron was hot. But this was not Longstreet's style; he preferred to get everything just so and then move slowly, so he ignored Lee's suggestion and took his time about organizing his move. He delayed so long that night fell and it was not until the next day that he finally went into action. When he did, all was forgiven, for he fell upon Pope's forces and scattered them. As with the previous battle, Second Bull Run ended with the discomfited Union troops fleeing towards Washington pell-mell, leaving 14,000 dead and wounded behind them, compared to a Confederate loss of 9000.

Second Bull Run was close call; another day would have seen an enormous Union reinforcement from McClellan's army. As it was, the late arrival of these forces was enough to prevent Jackson's cavalry from chasing Pope's tail into Washington. Lincoln despaired, Pope was banished to the West to fight Indians, and McClellan was brought back to Washington.

Lee now decided to carry the fight into the enemy's territory. He planned an advance on Harrisburg, Pennsylvania, with the intention of destroying the long railroad bridge across the Susquehanna River so as to cut a vital Union supply line. He hoped, too, that a foray into Maryland would bring the inhabitants of that state to declare for the Confederacy, after which, in Lee's words, "I will turn my attention to Philadelphia, Baltimore or Washington, as may seem best . . . . " There is also reason to believe that Lee felt that if this maneuver was a success it would put the Confederacy into a strong position to bargain for peace.

Three days after Second Bull Run, Lee's troops crossed the Potomac River into Maryland, bands playing and flags flying. At Frederick the army paused, and Lee decided to split his force, sending Jackson down to deal with the Union garrison at Harper's Ferry, while he, with Longstreet, pushed on towards Hagerstown, Maryland. Unfortunately, a discarded copy of Lee's orders was found by Union troops who followed into Frederick, and Lee's plans were soon known to McClellan who, for all his temerity, had enough sense to see when opportunity was handed to him on a plate. He immediately set his army marching towards the gap between Lee's two armies and despatched a corps southward to come up behind Stonewall Jackson's forces at Harper's Ferry.

**Left:** *The Second Battle of Bull Run was a disaster for the Union forces, which fled toward Washington leaving 14,000 dead and wounded.*

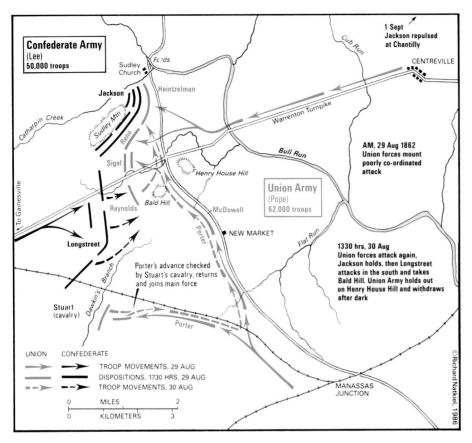

Confederate Army
(Lee)
**50,000 troops**

Above: *Map of Second Bull Run, a Confederate victory, fought August 29-30, 1862.*

Above right: *Union General John Pope.*

Below: *Map of the battle of Antietam, September 17, 1862, considered by many to be the bloodiest single day of the war. Lee took almost 14,000 casualties and McClellan 12,000.*

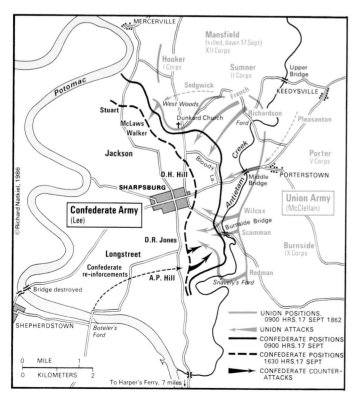

Confederate Army
(Lee)

On September 13 Lee was in camp at Hagerstown when he was told that McClellan's army was hot on his heels, pushing General J. E. B. Stuart's cavalry screen in front of it and making for Turner's Gap, the only feasible crossing of the mountains between Frederick and Hagerstown. Lee immediately sent orders for D. H. Hill to try and hold McClellan at Turner's Gap and for Longstreet to turn about and march to Hill's aid. Longstreet argued, but this time Lee brooked no argument, led Longstreet's column to the mountains and threw them straight into action to support the hard-pressed Hill. The Gap was held for the day, but Lee realized that McClellan had a third fresh corps ready to fling at him in the morning and there was no choice except to withdraw under the cover of darkness.

While he was considering this, Lee was given more bad news: McClellan's other corps, under General William Franklin, had crossed Crampton's Gap further south and by morning would be threatening Jackson at Harper's Ferry. That was enough for Lee; sizing things up in a realistic manner, he realized that his only course lay in abandoning his Maryland campaign forthwith. He would retreat west by way of Sharpsburg, Maryland, cross the Potomac and then move down to link up with Jackson, after which the reunited army would gradually pull back into Virginia.

Yet again a messenger appeared to change things; now came word from Jackson that he was confident Harper's Ferry would fall next morning. So Lee changed his plan slightly; he would still retire to Sharpsburg but there stand fast to await the arrival of Jackson, and between them they might well see McClellan off once more.

Lee rode to Sharpsburg on September 15 with about 20,000 survivors of Longstreet's and D. H. Hill's corps, and took up a position along the Antietam Creek. He was cheered by a message from Jackson to say that he had indeed taken Harper's Ferry, with 11,000 Union prisoners, 73 cannons and 13,000 rifles, and that he would join Lee on the following day. Meanwhile McClellan reverted to his usual cautious self and it was not until late in the afternoon that the first Union troops appeared across the Creek, fired a few rounds of cannon and then settled down for the night.

The next day opened with Union artillery fire but little else; McClellan was at his interminable business of getting everything just so before making a move, so that nothing had happened by the time that Jackson arrived at midday. Lee fed Jackson's men into his defensive line between Sharpsburg and Antietam Creek; on the right flank was General Longstreet and on the left General D. H. Hill and General John B. Hood's brigades. During the afternoon a Union advance by General Joseph Hooker's corps crossed the creek out of cannon range and probed at Hood's flank. The attack was not driven home and appeared to be little more than a reconnaissance in force. Night fell and Lee withdrew Hood's men for rest and replaced them with three of Jackson's brigades.

At three o'clock next morning, the 17th, the Union artillery opened fire and Hooker's corps attacked in earnest. Lee immediately roused Hood's men and sent them to assist. At the same time more Union artillery bombarded Jackson's position in the center of the line. By 6 AM Hood's men had thrown the Union attack back, but a counterattack drove in the Confederate lines, and confused hand-to-hand fighting broke out. By mid-morning the two sides had fought themselves to a standstill; Hood's troops were worn out and so were Hooker's. But the Union side had more fresh troops to throw in, and Lee was hard-pressed to move his forces to meet the threats as they developed. About 11 o'clock, how-

ever, came a ray of hope; Jackson had left Confederate General Lafayette McLaws and his corps at Harper's Ferry, to make their own way to Sharpsburg – they had been on the north side of the Potomac at Harper's Ferry – and now they appeared, weary and tired after their forced march. Weary or not, they were thrown straight into battle. As luck would have it they appeared in a gap between two Confederate positions, into which a formidable Union attack was advancing. With Confederates on three sides, this turned into a fatal cul-de-sac, and 220 Union men died instantly.

Now it was the turn of Hill's corps to be overrun; a misheard order led a regiment to fall back, the Union troops opposite seized the chance and swooped in, causing other Confederate units to fall away. The situation was saved only by a battery of guns opening fire at point-blank range with case shot, stopping the Union rush for long enough to get some infantry into place. This was the turning point of the day; General Edwin Sumner, the opposing Union commander, had seen his troops cut to pieces and now, through the smoke and dust, he saw what appeared to be Confederate reinforcements moving up; they were not – they were simply disordered fragments of battered regiments being moved around to plug gaps – but the sight was

**Below:** *General Robert E. Lee watching the fighting at Antietam, in an engraving from a drawing by the Civil War artist Alfred R. Waud.*

**Right:** *General Burnside's Union troops made a gallant charge over the bridge at midday but were pushed back by A. P. Hill's forces.*

The rebels covered by a ledge of rock repulsing the troops on the right — in the woods beyond the Dunker ch. antietam

**Left:** *A sketch by A. R. Waud of a line of Confederate soldiers at Antietam.*

**Overleaf:** *Federal forces advancing under fire at the battle of Antietam.*

enough to convince Sumner that his efforts were useless. He withheld further attacks and advised McClellan of his opinions and action.

McClellan was not dismayed; he was unaware that if Sumner had thrown the fresh corps he had ready, there is little doubt it would have carried the day and ended the battle there and then. But McClellan thought that Lee's force was unbalanced, concentrated in his center and left. Southward, Burnside and a strong Union force had crossed the creek on Lee's right flank and appeared to have nothing very much between them and Sharpsburg. In McClellan's view, that was the decisive flank and there the battle would be won.

Burnside's crossing had not been easy; two Georgia regiments had held him up for half the day before they finally gave way. By that time Lee had managed to move three brigades to cover his flank, and they, and the remnants of the Georgians and South Carolinans, did what they could to delay Burnside's advance.

Into this threatening situation, shortly before four in the afternoon, came the final miracle. A. P. Hill's corps had been left at Harper's Ferry to secure the supplies there and attend to prisoners. Finishing his task, Hill then put his men on the road for Sharpsburg and now, at the proverbial eleventh hour, they appeared, having marched from Harper's Ferry in seven hours. Their line of approach enabled them to fall straight upon the exposed flank of Burnside's columns, and that was enough; the Union troops broke and fell back across the creek. And as suddenly as that the Battle of Sharpsburg – or Antietam – was over.

Darkness fell and both sides attended to the enormous number of dead and wounded. The next day Lee and his battered army sat tight and waited for McClellan, while McClellan and his battered army sat and waited for Lee. But

**Above:** *Dead Confederate artillerymen lying in the sunken road known as Bloody Lane, after a Union attack at Antietam.*

**Right:** *With Union morale on the upswing after Antietam, President Lincoln presented the Emancipation Proclamation.*

there was no other course for the Confederates except dignified retreat, and Lee marched what was left of his army across the Potomac and back into Virginia.

Tactically, Antietam was a draw; strategically, it was a Confederate loss, for it saw an end to their proposed Maryland campaign. What was more vital was that it sapped the strength of the Confederates, for Antietam was the bloodiest battle of the entire war. Lee lost 2700 dead, 9024 wounded and 2000 missing: 13,724 casualties from a total strength of 51,844 – almost 27 percent. McClellan's losses were 2108 dead, 9549 wounded and 753 missing: 12,410 casualties from a strength of 75,316 – just over 16 percent. The difference was that the Union had an almost unlimited pool of manpower from which to make good their loss; the Confederates did not.

The other effect of Antietam was to raise Union morale, which had slumped after the Seven Days and Second Bull Run, and it also gave Lincoln the opportunity to deliver his Emancipation Proclamation. This changed the war aim from simply dealing with secession to a more moral campaign to crush slavery, a shift which very rapidly removed what sympathy the Confederates had been able to raise in Europe. Supporting revolutionaries was one thing; supporting slavery was something else, and the Europeans had no wish to be associated with it.

# Fredericksburg

After Antietam there was the usual lull while the two sides collected their wits and decided what to do next. Lincoln, finally tiring of McClellan's style of operations, retired him and selected General Burnside as his replacement. Lee was sorry to see McClellan go; he knew McClellan's ways and could usually foresee what his reaction would be to any situation. Now he would have to learn Burnside's style and adjust to it. Fortunately for Lee, Burnside had very little style; for all his martial appearance he was incompetent, so

incompetent that it took some time for Lee to realize that what appeared to be devious moves by Burnside were usually nothing more than stupid ones.

In order to recuperate, Lee had moved his forces back to where supplies were available and the men could rest and eat. Jackson was in the Shenandoah Valley, and Longstreet at Culpeper, Virginia. Burnside, in accordance with instructions from Lincoln, now pointed his army toward Richmond and set off in a straight line, aiming first for Fredericksburg,

**Right:** *Union Major General Ambrose E. Burnside, depicted at Fredericksburg, where he is generally considered to have made a poor showing. Lee believed him incompetent.*

**Above:** *Union troops crossing the Rappahannock River at Fredericksburg as engineers lay pontoon bridges. Union delays in crossing gave Lee plenty of time to prepare a strong defense.*

**Left:** *A sketch by artist A. R. Waud showing General McClellan, accompanied by General Burnside, taking leave of the Union Army of the Potomac. Lee regretted McClellan's departure, having found him so predictable.*

Virginia, and a crossing of the Rappahannock River. Lee, at first, could scarcely believe this; in his view Burnside's logical course was to head for Culpeper and destroy Longstreet, since the object of war is to destroy the enemy's army in the field, not merely occupy his capital city. He was sure that there was more to it than this; he suspected that what Burnside had in mind was putting his army onto the water and floating down the Rappahannock to land below Richmond and make a flank attack. It is doubtful if Burnside ever imagined such a thing. Lee despatched Jeb Stuart's cavalry on reconnaissance, and eventually was convinced that what he saw was what there was: Burnside was going to cross the river at Fredericksburg and advance on Richmond, as simply as that.

Fredericksburg was not a good place to oppose a river crossing; the bluffs on the north bank gave Union artillery excellent command of the south bank, thus preventing effective action. Lee preferred a position on Marye's Heights about a mile south of the town, from where he could mount a firm defense, but the basic problem was that this left him no room to maneuver and counterattack. He could stop Burnside, but not defeat him. He would really have preferred to establish his line even further south, on the North Anna River, where he had room to move and capitalize on his ability to stop Burnside. On the other hand, the further south he made his stand, the more productive farmland,

and its produce, he was giving away to Burnside. So it had to be Marye's Heights.

Longstreet's corps moved across from Culpeper on November 19; Lee did not order Jackson to move until November 26, since he had left Jackson as long as he dared in order to resist any Union movement in the Valley. The delay was not vital; Burnside had halted his leading elements at Falmouth, across the river from Fredericksburg, instructing them to await the arrival of bridging trains. This took almost three weeks, during which time Lee was able to prepare his positions with care. At this point the changing nature of war revealed itself; the Union general, Sumner, sent a message to the civilian population to evacuate Fredericksburg or suffer the consequences when artillery began bombarding the town. On Lee's advice the civilians, with their bundles of belongings, moved out, in a snowstorm. Lee then posted sharpshooters in the abandoned town to hold up the Union bridging operation for as long as possible.

These "Barksdale's Mississippians" – so-called since they were from Ethelbert Barksdale's brigade of 17th and 18th Mississippi Regiments – were called to action early on December 11 as the sounds of Burnside's pontoon builders came faintly through the foggy darkness. Firing merely at the sounds, they drove off the pioneers 10 times, until by the early afternoon Burnside, his patience exhausted, opened fire on the city with 181 guns, the heaviest massed artillery fire of the war so far. This covered the final attempt of the pioneers, and by late afternoon Union troops were crossing the completed bridges and advancing into the ruins of Fredericksburg, with Barksdale's men slowly falling back and delaying the invasion.

On the following day and night the remainder of the Union army crossed the river, followed by their formidable artillery strength. During this period Lee carefully arrayed his forces across the ridge line south and west of Fredericksburg and amidst thick woodlands to the east, ensured they had built effective defensive parapets, and took up his position more or less centrally. All the Confederate troops now had to do was wait for the Union army to come within shooting range.

On the morning of December 13 a fog concealed everything below the Confederate positions, and at 10 o'clock the wintry sun finally shone through and revealed Burnside's 100,000-man army aligned and dressed as for review, steadily advancing towards Lee's defenders. The battle opened with an artillery duel of formidable proportions, but this eased as the infantry crept closer. The initial Union advance on Lee's right flank was thrown back with heavy losses, but the oncoming horde merely changed their axis slightly and moved inexorably towards the heights where Lee stood. As the Union forces came closer, so Jackson's corps began pouring bullets from their commanding position and this withering fire, together with well-directed artillery, simply dissolved the Union ranks.

At about noon the axis of Burnside's advance changed

**Left:** *Burnside's soldiers advancing in the open toward Fredericksburg's defenders. Lee's men were well protected on the ridge line and poured withering fire down upon the hapless attackers.*

**Below:** *The attacking Union troops crossing the Rappahannock were picked off by Confederate sharpshooters stationed in the town.*

and the "Grand Division" of some 27,000 men appeared from the ruins of Fredericksburg, formed into battle lines on a plateau in front of Marye's Heights, and then marched towards the Confederate lines. At this point, according to several independent observers, the battlefield simply became a slaughterhouse. The Confederates were securely in place behind a sunken road and a stone wall, amply supported by artillery and liberally provided with ammunition, while the Union troops were struggling uphill into this storm of lead. Nine thousand Union troops fell on the slopes, not one of them ever reaching the Confederate position. It was this scene which led to Lee's famous remark: "It is well war is so terrible. We should grow too fond of it."

Burnside, across the river, was stricken with despair at the carnage and wildly announced that he would go across, take charge of his old corps and lead the attack in person, but he was dissuaded by his staff from such a suicidal course. Eventually, he withdrew his troops back across the river, leaving behind an estimated 13,000 dead and wounded. Confederate casualties were scarcely 5000, mostly lightly wounded.

The victory was Lee's but it was an inconclusive one; he hoped that Burnside would renew his attack, so that the Union army would be so severely depleted as to render it ineffective for months to come, but Burnside had had enough and withdrew behind the river, after his troops had thoroughly sacked Fredericksburg and looted everything portable. A counterattack by Lee was impossible, due to the

**Left:** *The sunken road and stone wall on Marye's Heights from which the well protected Confederates halted the Union assault on Fredericksburg. This photograph was taken months later, after the hill was finally taken by Union General John Sedgwick's 6th Maine Infantry.*

**Overleaf:** *Wounded soldiers on Marye's Heights. Amputation was a common treatment for bullet wounds, and only one in seven wounded soldiers would survive.*

dominating positions of Burnside's artillery across the river. Both armies did the only thing possible in the circumstances; they went into winter quarters, more concerned with staying warm than with fighting.

Burnside's poor showing at Fredericksburg led to his replacement; the new commander of the Army of the Potomac was General Joseph Hooker. Hooker was not short of confidence, and had pulled every possible string to obtain the post. It has to be admitted that he did a magnificent job of reviving the morale of the Union army, reorganizing the formations, improving the food and medical arrangements, organizing furloughs and generally pulling the Army of the Potomac together. There was no doubt in his mind that he would crush the Confederacy; "When I get to Richmond" soon became "After I have taken Richmond".

Meanwhile Lee was suffering from a poor supply system which was failing to provide the basic rations and stores needed by his army; complaints to Jefferson Davis did no good, and eventually it was to be discovered that the superintendent of the Richmond, Fredericksburg & Potomac Railroad was, in fact, a Union spy. But at this point all Lee knew was that the supplies were not getting through and his army was suffering. At the same time Lee was doing his best to reorganize the staff of his army. His own staff he now had the way he wanted, but the staffs of the various corps and divisions were far less efficient and Lee urged some reforms on Davis, notably the formation of a staff corps, but, like most of his suggestions, it was ignored.

# Chancellorsville

As the bitter winter drew to a close, "Fighting Joe" Hooker finally made a move. Lee was waiting for this, and had assessed the Union's options. The basic Union need was to get out of their position on the Rappahannock so as to obtain room to maneuver, and the only way to achieve this would be for Hooker to move west and try to outflank Lee; an eastern flanking movement was impossible due to the swamps and widening of the river.

But before Hooker moved, there was another threat to be considered when the Union 9th Corps landed at Newport News, Virginia. Lee speculated that their aim could be to attack North Carolina in support of Union inland operations or to advance on the south side of the James River so as to threaten Petersburg and outflank Richmond.

To try and contain this threat, Lee dispatched General Longstreet with two divisions, those of General Hood and General George E. Pickett, and sent him south to resist any Union advance while remaining close to the railroad near Richmond so as to be able to move rapidly back if recalled. In addition, he was to send out foraging parties to build up the army's stock of food, and generally supervise the defensive positions from the James River to North Carolina.

This was a mistake on Lee's part; Longstreet was jealous of Jackson's successes and was anxious to make a name for himself as an independent commander. So with 40,000 troops under his command he saw his opportunity for fame and pestered Lee with demands for more troops so that he could take the offensive against the Union forces, even suggesting that Lee retreat to a defensive position so as to yield more troops up to Longstreet's planned offensive.

As usual, Lee replied in a gentle and noncommittal manner, which did nothing to discourage Longstreet, and at the end of March, when Burnside re-embarked his 9th Corps from Newport News in order to send them west, Lee gently suggested that it was about time Longstreet came back and

rejoined the main army. It is generally assumed that Lee's lack of authority here stemmed from a debilitating illness from which he was suffering at the time; plagued by pains in his chest, back and arms, and with a throat infection, Lee simply did not have the energy to act decisively with Longstreet, who now set out on a futile and pointless siege of the town of Suffolk, Virginia.

The error of allowing Longstreet his head became apparent on April 29, when Hooker moved. He had what he called "the finest army on the planet," a total of 138,378 men under arms with which to attack Lee and his total of 62,000. Hooker began his move by launching a 40,000-strong attack straight across the Rappahannock at Fredericksburg, in the same manner as Burnside. Lee considered this, conferred with Jackson and his other commanders, and decided that this was a feint and that Hooker would make his major attack some distance to the west. Leaving a single corps to contain the Union attack, Lee moved the rest of his army to the west, trying to discern where Hooker would make his attack. At the same time he wired to Richmond that all available forces should be sent to him immediately; the Adjutant General forwarded a telegraph message to Longstreet, directing him to return to Lee's command as soon as possible. Three days later, Longstreet wrote back: "I cannot move unless the entire force is moved . . . it would take several days to reach Fredericksburg . . . I will endeavour to move as soon as possible. . . ." Lee was going to fight Hooker with a quarter of his army sitting idle, miles from the battle.

Jeb Stuart's cavalry soon informed Lee that Hooker had crossed the Rapidan River at two points and was advancing towards Fredericksburg from the northwest, so that Lee was now between two Union armies. On the morning of April 30 the advance guards of the two sides met at a clearing west of Fredericksburg called Chancellorsville, on the

edge of a heavily wooded area known locally as "The Wilderness." Hooker moved his headquarters into the Chancellor family house; Lee's leading troops under Major General Richard H. Anderson fell back and prepared a defensive line while Lee rushed the major part of his army to join them.

Lee had two advantages; firstly, Hooker had sent most of his cavalry off on destructive raids, so that he had only one brigade left to act as a reconnaissance force, while Lee had Jeb Stuart and 5000 horsemen as his eyes and ears.

Secondly, the Wilderness area was a factor overlooked by Hooker and one which would prevent observation and effective fire from the Union artillery. Lee therefore decided to attack Hooker, and having made sure that the activity around Fredericksburg was only a diversion, rode off to Chancellorsville to find that a strange situation had developed.

Hooker had moved his forces forward of the Wilderness, largely so that his artillery could have open fields of fire. His forces were poised to sweep forward and overwhelm Lee –

**Left:** *In his belief that the Confederate army was retreating, Union General "Fighting Joe" Hooker moved his huge force to the west of Fredericksburg toward Chancellorsville.*

**Above:** *Jeb Stuart was Lee's eyes and ears at the battle of Chancellorsville. When Jackson was wounded, Stuart was given his command.*

**Above right:** *Union General Joseph Hooker, commander of the Army of the Potomac, was outmaneuvered and outfought by Lee at Chancellorsville.*

and they quite probably would have done so. And then Hooker's nerve failed. This blustering general who had promised to crush Lee and his pitiful army was seized by a fit of depression, terrified by distant guns, prey to every kind of doubt. Without any warning he suddenly ordered an immediate withdrawal from the open positions to take up defensive positions within the protection of the Wilderness woods.

His generals could scarcely believe their ears; they argued, but to no avail, and like good soldiers they had to obey. But the move took the spirit out of the entire Union army; even the humblest soldier could see that they had been ready to end the war at a stroke, and now they were falling back.

Lee, too, could scarcely believe his ears when he heard that four Union corps had retreated in the face of five Confederate divisions. He suspected a trap, or some devious maneuver. After analyzing the situation and realizing what was happening, he rapidly reconnoitered the Union positions, finding that the enemy on his right had wisely pulled tight against the Rappahannock River and fortified their position with felled trees and obstacles. After a quick evening conference with Jackson, Lee sent two engineer officers

**Right:** *Hooker's army under attack by the Confederates in the Wilderness. Severely punished in both the front and rear, Hooker withdrew from Chancellorsville and then, threatened by Lee's united forces, recrossed the Rappahannock. Robert E. Lee had defeated a Union force several times the strength of his own.*

off to study Hooker's right flank, and they soon returned to announce that the Union's line ended in thin air in the Wilderness without being anchored by any specific physical feature.

Once armed with this knowledge, Lee soon saw his advantage; he would send Jackson south to a convenient road, then west and north until he had outflanked the Union position and could fall upon Hooker's rear, the march being protected by a screen of Stuart's cavalry. When appraised of this plan Jackson fell in with it at once, and outdid Lee in audacity by proposing to take his whole corps, leaving Lee

no more than a couple of under-strength divisions to face the major part of the Union army. This also meant that Lee would have to command this force, since his divisional generals were not competent to face Hooker without Lee's guiding hand. Nevertheless, he agreed, and at 4 AM on May 1, Jackson moved.

Jackson's movements in the early morning light were seen by a Union battery, which opened fire, but Jackson moved his column to another road – still known today as "Jackson's Trail" – and kept moving. In order to find out what was going on, two Union divisions from Major General

Daniel E. Sickles' 3rd Corps advanced, driving back a Confederate outpost. Jackson sent back some troops, and, aided by others already in position on the other side of the inroad, the Union force was quickly ambushed and driven out. By three in the afternoon, driving forward in the hot sun, Jackson had his men positioned directly in the rear of Hooker's army and, guided by Lee's cavalryman son Fitzhugh Lee, was quietly overlooking an encampment of Union troops sprawling in the sun, smoking and eating, secure in the knowledge that they were well behind the line.

Using concealed routes, Jackson moved up two divi-

sions, and by 6 PM had them in position overlooking the encampment. He then turned them loose, and 18,000 howling men burst from the woods and descended on the Union camp. Two Union divisions gave way immediately and simply fled the field; a third, further back, attempted to take up positions to repel the attack but were foiled by the fleeing bodies of their own side, and soon gave way. Hooker's right flank had been disintegrated within an hour.

When the sounds of Jackson's battle reached him, Lee immediately turned to the attack, less with the hope of actually gaining victory than with the intention of simply

**Left:** *General Lee leading his triumphant troops at Chancellorsville. After the battle, Lee could look out on a Virginia free of Union forces from the Wilderness to Richmond.*

**Above:** *A postwar depiction of the last meeting between Robert E. Lee and Stonewall Jackson at Chancellorsville. The victory there belonged as much to Jackson as to his commander.*

pinning down the Union troops on his front so that they could not disengage and fall back to help Hooker.

Meanwhile Jackson, flushed with victory, planned to send A. P. Hill's six brigades into the line to replace those which had made the initial Confederate attack. Riding through the darkness, Jackson's party was confronted by artillery fire, so they turned about and galloped back, attempting to get out of range of the Union guns. In the woods alongside the road lay the 18th North Carolina regiment and they, in the darkness, took the sound of horses to be a Union cavalry attack and opened fire. Jackson was hit in the hand and arm by three bullets, severing a main artery. He was hurried through shell fire to a field hospital where his arm was amputated.

When Lee was informed of Jackson's wounds – before the amputation was known of – tears sprang to his eyes. "Any victory is dearly bought which deprives us of the services of General Jackson, even for a short time," he said. But in spite

of his distress he turned immediately to the problem of picking up where Jackson had been forced to leave off. A. P. Hill had also been wounded and the forward troops had no inkling of what Jackson had planned. Lee therefore gave Jackson's command to Jeb Stuart with orders to drive forward and unite the two portions of Lee's army, since the opportunity to completely cut off Hooker had now passed.

Hooker had made another error during the night by withdrawing some of his artillery from a commanding position; Stuart spotted this and directed Confederate artillery to the position so that it could rake the Union lines and this, together with spirited Confederate attacks, led Hooker to pull back even further and set up a defensive line so that he was now in a triangular area, one flank resting on the Rappahannock and the other on the Rapidan River. And under Stuart's inspiring leadership the western element of the Confederates pushed forward around the apex of Hooker's position until they met the advance guards of Anderson's force which had been left behind when Jackson made his flanking movement. Lee's army was, once again, a single unit; his immense gamble of splitting his forces had succeeded.

Hooker fell back from Chancellorsville, but the Union forces at Fredericksburg had finally managed to drive the Confederates out of their defensive positions. The Confederates fell back southward as they had been instructed, but this allowed Sedgwick's Union force to move west so as to take the pressure off Hooker. This was achieved, since Lee was forced to break off his attacks in order to send two

brigades back to stave off Sedgwick's advance. On the following day, Lee determined that Hooker was too securely positioned to be moved, so he decided to finish off Sedgwick instead. Anderson was deployed around Sedgwick's flank, and Brigadier General Jubal Early, with the troops which had moved southward from Fredericksburg, now returned to threaten Sedgwick's rear. Caught on three sides, Sedgwick rapidly turned about and crossed the Rappahannock to safety.

Lee now gathered his forces together and deployed them for one last drive at Hooker, but Fighting Joe didn't wait to argue; during heavy rain on the night of May 5, he withdrew his troops across the Rappahannock, and when day dawned there was nothing in front of Lee's army except the river. Against all the odds and precepts of warfare, Lee had defeated a force three times his own strength; it was undoubtedly his masterpiece. Unfortunately, for Lee the pleasure was completely ruined by the death of Stonewall Jack-

**Above:** *General Stonewall Jackson at Chancellorsville. His death from complications of a wound received there deprived the South of a daring soldier.*

**Right:** *Confederate General Stonewall Jackson posed for this photograph by Mathew Brady in late April 1863, only two weeks before the General's death.*

son; after the amputation pneumonia supervened, and, after lingering for a week, Jackson died on May 10. Lee wept; he had not only lost a friend, he had lost his most reliable general, a man with whom he could plan and execute maneuvers of any degree of complexity, secure in the knowledge that his orders would be understood and carried out. Without Jackson it is doubtful if Lee could have won at Chancellorsville; and without Jackson it was almost certain that nothing so daring could ever be attempted again.

# Gettysburg

After Chancellorsville, General Longstreet belatedly returned to Lee with his two divisions. Lee had lost 13,000 men at Chancellorsville, and even with Longstreet's return he now had barely 40,000 infantry. In addition his entire army was destitute and short of food, a circumstance which meant that the prime reason for maneuver would now be that of obtaining supplies from some area which had not already been ravaged and stripped. Davis wanted to take portions of Lee's army and send them west to save Vicksburg, Mississippi under attack by General U. S. Grant. Since Lee could not persuade Davis and the Richmond authorities to provide food and clothing, he had to persuade Davis that stripping away part of his force to defend Vicksburg would be futile; in the first place there was no guarantee that they would be sufficient to turn the scales there, and in the second place it would leave Lee so short of troops as to give him no alternative but to fall back on the lines around Richmond and await the inevitable Union siege. Like most amateur strategists Davis could not bear the thought of giving up all the ground so hardly won, and he therefore listened rather more receptively when Lee outlined a different strategy.

Lee's idea was simple; to invade the North, where supplies could be obtained, and thus draw the Union forces

away from ideas of advancing against Richmond. To do this, of course, he would need to have all his various detached units returned to his main army, and also a force from North Carolina would be required to move up into Virginia so as to form a threat to Washington while Lee was making his northward advance, so keeping a large proportion of the Union Army tied down protecting the capital.

Davis saw the sense of Lee's proposed northward advance, but that was as far as his comprehension went. During the year that Lee had been in the field, away from Richmond, his influence on Davis had declined, and Davis was obsessed with his own theories which involved spreading troops all over the South in small garrisons. He had a very orderly mind, which was at its best when drawing up impressive tables of organization and diagrams of troop deployment, and having gotten the troops to match the paperwork Davis was not inclined to disturb his careful and symmetrical arrangements. Moreover his dispositions conflicted with those which Lee wanted to make. In the aftermath of Chancellorsville, Lee had to reorganize his army because there was no replacement general who was good enough, as Jackson had been, to command a four-division corps. Lee therefore had to reorganize into three corps instead of two, using generals and staff officers known and tried. At this juncture Davis stepped in and began taking troops out of Lee's force and replacing them with untried troops led by unblooded officers. Davis was unable to

*Rebel cavalry cross the Potomac into Maryland on June 11, 1863. Lee had decided to invade the North in order to replenish his supplies and to forestall further Federal advances on Richmond.*

**Above:** *Artist's sketch of the destruction of the railroad bridge by fleeing Union soldiers as General Lee's army occupies Wrightsville, Pennsylvania, June 28, 1863. Lee was moving toward the town of Gettysburg, as was George Meade's Union Army of the Potomac.*

**Right:** *General Robert E. Lee discovered at Gettysburg that the kind of organized operations he had conducted with the help of Stonewall Jackson were no longer possible. Confederate plans for concerted action failed repeatedly during the three-day battle.*

**Right:** *General George Meade replaced Hooker as commander of the Union Army of the Potomac a few days before Gettysburg. Lee recognized that General Meade posed a serious threat.*

understand the intangible matter of morale and the cohesion which automatically came from an army composed of units which had already fought together and trusted each other. And to crown all this, Davis insisted on taking out more elements to provide guard units for Richmond.

In the end Lee eventually realized that the Davis line was simply that Lee could do what he liked with whatever troops he had, but he was not going to receive any reinforcements via Davis, and no changes to Davis' beloved charts would be made in order to support Lee. And so when Lee finally ordered his army to move northward on June 3, he did so with a heavy heart. He no longer had Jackson, he no longer had the unquestioning support of the Confederate Government, he no longer had a finely-tuned and cohesive army; he no longer had the hope of final victory either. He was moving because he had to move or starve; it was as simple as that.

Lee's advance led him to the western side of the Blue Ridge Mountains, and he instructed – rather than ordered – Jeb Stuart to protect his right flank, either by guarding the mountain passes to Lee's east or, if he preferred, by crossing the mountains to act as a screen between Lee and the Army of the Potomac. Unfortunately, Stuart had recently suffered a blow to his self-esteem; his cavalry had met a force of Union cavalry near Brandy Station, just south of the Rappahannock, and had very nearly been defeated. This was the first time Stuart had even got close to being beaten, and his enemies were not slow in suggesting that perhaps

Stuart wasn't quite so smart as he thought he was. And so, instead of attending closely to Lee's instructions, Stuart fell into the same trap as Longstreet and saw his chance to go glory-hunting. First he attempted to ride around Hooker's army; then, since Hooker's movement northward prevented this, he set off into Maryland and captured a Union wagon train. This would provide the necessary glory, and he set off back to rejoin Lee; but slowly, since he had to shepherd the 125 captured wagons along.

This was all very fine for Stuart, but Lee was blind and deaf without his cavalry reconnaissance. He reached Chambersburg, Pennsylvania, and camped there, waiting anxiously to hear from Stuart as to what Hooker was up to. And in the evening a spy came to inform him that two Union corps were just across the mountains from Lee and knew where he was; and that Hooker had resigned and had been replaced by General George C. Meade. Both elements of this intelligence dismayed Lee: firstly, two Union corps who knew where he was formed a serious threat; and secondly, Meade was not of the same breed as Hooker or McClellan. As Lee said, Meade was the type of general who would not make mistakes, and who, if Lee made a mistake, would be quick to take advantage of it.

Lee sent A. P. Hill's corps across the mountains to see what they could discover of the Union strength. On the following day came a report that one of Hill's brigades had headed for the small town of Gettysburg on hearing that there might be some shoes to be had, and en route had bumped into some Union cavalry and retired to Cashtown at the foot of the mountains. Lee was not unduly perturbed about this, since it was inevitable that cavalry patrols would be met. But the Union patrol commander was alert and had informed Meade of his encounter, and by the next day, July 1, the Army of the Potomac was on the march towards Gettysburg.

On that same morning Hill's brigade set out once more to find the shoes they heard were in Gettysburg, followed by the rest of their division. Unfortunately most of this force were new troops under untried officers; they ran into the Union flank just outside Gettysburg, the two leading brigades were severely mauled, and Major General Henry Heth, divisional commander, just managed to put his other two brigades into position. And so, by default, by the absence of Confederate cavalry and by the want of shoes for the soldiers, the battle of Gettysburg was about to begin.

Lee was crossing the mountains when he heard the firing, and hastened forward to see what was happening. He arrived at Heth's position, surveyed the scene and then saw Union troops moving out from Gettysburg with the obvious intent of assaulting Heth. But just at that moment a Confederate division under General R. E. Rodes appeared over the horizon from the north; this was part of General Richard S. Ewell's force which had originally set off in the direction of Harrisburg but which had been recalled by Lee two days before. Now they appeared providentially on the field just at the time and place Lee needed them.

Rodes was a good commander, and as soon as he heard firing to his front he had deployed his division off the road and onto a parallel ridge. Here they encountered the Union German corps, and things began to look bad. Then another stroke of providence brought General Jubal Early's division, another outposted force which Lee had called in, marching on a line which brought him precisely to the flank of the at-tacking Union troops. Jubal Early did not hesitate, but threw his troops straight at the target in front of him. Lee, who had watched these unforeseen arrivals with considerable relief, now ordered Heth to attack with his two brigades, plus a third division which had arrived in support. The Union troops were now under attack from three directions; the German corps gave way and, outflanked, the remainder of the Union troops fell back into Gettysburg, followed by troops from Ewell's divisions, who took 5000 prisoners en route.

The Union forces passed through the town and took up positions on a hill south of the town, on the crest of which was a cemetery. Lee asked Hill if his men could advance from their ridge, flanking the hill, and seize it. Hill thought his men too tired and short of ammunition. Lee then sent a message to Ewell to take the hill, but added the fatal clause "if practicable." Lee then waited all afternoon for Ewell to move, but nothing happened, and toward evening he set out for Ewell's headquarters. When he got there, as darkness was falling, he soon realized that Ewell's nerve had failed him and he had never given the order to take Cemetery Hill.

It seemed as if the nerve had gone from all his commanders; Ewell, Rode, even Jubal Early now found good reasons why an attack on the morrow would not be a good idea. It seemed that the fire had gone out under Jackson's old corps. Lee rode back to his own headquarters and spent the rest of the night puzzling how to deal with the Union position without having to place too much reliance on a substantial part of his force. He eventually decided to pull Ewell's corps round from the north of Gettysburg to a position under his command at Seminary Ridge and use them to support a morning attack. Orders were sent to Ewell, but to Lee's surprise the response was that Ewell himself rode over to see Lee and apologize for his former indecisiveness. Ewell agreed to attack from his present positions.

This cheered up Lee; now, with Ewell attacking from his left flank and Longstreet, then getting into position, attacking from the right, and Hill making threatening moves in the center, an attack seemed feasible, and a third division was available as a reserve, to be thrown in to reinforce whatever flank was successful. And to crown everything, news came that Jeb Stuart was just north at Carlisle, and would join him in the morning. "Gentlemen," said Lee, "we will attack the enemy as early in the morning as possible."

The dawn of July 2 found Lee with his troops ready on Seminary Ridge, facing across a shallow valley to Cemetery Hill and, about a mile and a half to the south, two hills called Little Round Top and Big Round Top. Between the ridge and Cemetery Hill was a wheatfield and a peach orchard; in front of the Round Tops the ground was marshy and strewn with boulders. The axis of the attack was northeast so as to avoid the difficult ground where possible.

Into this fairly simple plan Longstreet now inserted complications. He was, as revealed in his later writings, somewhat scornful of Lee's ability and felt that orders, when given to him, were no more than a basis for discussion. So he now appeared at Lee's side and proposed that instead of attacking, the Confederates should simply outflank Meade to the south and place themselves between Gettysburg and Washington, select a good defensive position, and there await attack. In fact Meade had already thought of this one and was hoping Lee would try it, having made preparations for such a move. Moreover it was an impractical maneuver for Lee since much of his force was still dispersed and he was extremely short of supplies. Lee merely listened to Longstreet and dismissed the whole idea without bothering to discuss it, turning, instead, to the immediate problem of getting the attack underway. Upon which Longstreet went back to his command determined to procrastinate until Lee could be made to see things his way.

Ewell made his attack in good style, but Longstreet sat fast, taking his time about moving his men. Eventually, once Longstreet's troops were underway, Lee simply said to him "I think you had better move on," and then rode off to see Ewell. He discovered that, once more, Ewell had run out of steam, but his men had secured good defensive positions in front of Gettysburg, so Lee was satisfied to leave him holding the line there until Longstreet made his attack, whereupon Ewell would make a demonstration which he was at liberty to turn into an attack if things looked favorable. Around 10 AM Lee started back to his post on Seminary Ridge.

By that time Longstreet's artillery should have been firing and his attack underway, but nothing was happening. Lee eventually found Longstreet and his staff tucked away in the woods, doing nothing. Lee immediately ordered him to attack, but even then Longstreet argued for delay, demanding to wait until the rearguard brigade had arrived. As they were due in 30 minutes, Lee agreed to the wait. In the event it was almost an hour before the troops arrived, and by the time they had taken a short rest and organized themselves it was well past noon when finally Longstreet's attack got underway, personally supervised by Lee. Once the troops were moving, Lee turned back to his command post; once Lee was out of sight Longstreet came to a halt.

Longstreet was at his happiest when conducting a defense; he was also happy when independent; he resented taking orders from Lee. And as a result he now threw the battle of Gettysburg away. Out of sheer pique at Lee's having given him brusque orders to attack, and at his ignoring Longstreet's proposals for evasive action, Longstreet now played the "spoiled brat" ploy; he obeyed to the letter everything Lee had ordered, even though he knew that conditions had changed and that those orders were no longer relevant. By the time that the dilatory Longstreet had got into position for the final attack, the Union lines now extended from Cemetery Hill to Little Round Top, and an

**Left:** *A view of the small town of Gettysburg and a Federal encampment as seen from Cemetery Hill.*

**Right:** *Longstreet's belated attack on the Union center was turned into a shambles by the defenders. Lee may not have known at this point how his plan was proceeding.*

oblique attack, as originally ordered, would expose Longstreet's flank to the Union left. But instead of informing Lee of the changed situation, Longstreet simply ordered his divisions to attack as ordered, in echelon. His subordinate generals pointed out that this was courting disaster, and suggested instead a flanking move around Little Round Top which would take the Union lines in reverse. Longstreet refused to consider this and insisted that "General Lee's orders are to attack up the Emmitsburg Road." This gambit, blaming a bad decision on somebody else, was another of Longstreet's favorite tactics.

The attack turned into a shambles, with troops doing their best to conform to orders which no longer made sense. Many troops reached their objectives, but they were so worn out that they were inevitably repulsed by the Union defenders. Senior officers were wounded and killed, so that units now had no commanders and were devoid of orders or information. Lee, isolated on his hilltop and blinded by cannon-smoke and dust, was unable to discern exactly what was going on and simply assumed that his generals were doing what he had told them to do. There is evidence to suggest that Lee was ill with a stomach complaint that day, but whatever the cause, he was not his usual observant self, and he let the battle rage without attempting any form of control. And due to this, regiments were struggling and dying while divisions sat idle on the outskirts of the battle, lacking orders to go in and support. What Lee was begin-

ning to realize was that the operations he had conducted with the aid of Jackson were simply no longer possible.

Eventually darkness came and the troops rested where they lay; Lee returned to his tent and planned the next day's moves. Although the Union line had not been broken, it had been severely strained, and provided Lee could get his army moving together, it seemed likely that a frontal attack at the Union center, supported by all his artillery, might be decisive. At dawn, Lee rode to Longstreet's camp and told him what he planned; Longstreet argued, now bringing out the threat of flanking from the Union lines which he had ignored on the previous day. Better, he said, to wait until a fresh division, under General Pickett, arrived and joined Hill's forces to strike at the center. Lee, probably by now tired of argument, wearily agreed.

**Below:** *The hill known as Little Round Top formed one of the anchors of the Union lines. A proposal to move around the hill, rather than making a direct assault, was vetoed by Longstreet with disastrous results for the Confederate attackers.*

**Right:** *A depiction of the second day at Gettysburg shows Confederate troops facing a Union-held hill.*

**Right below:** *The third day of fighting at Gettysburg, depicting the final rout of the rebel forces on July 3, 1863.*

The plan was, once more, for concerted action; Ewell would attack on the left while Longstreet attacked in the right center. But again, it all went wrong: Ewell attacked bravely, Longstreet failed to move, Ewell was beaten back, Longstreet still failed to move. Just before noon a fearsome artillery duel sprang up as Longstreet's artillery tried to beat down the Union defenses prior to the final assault, and the ensuing bombardment was one of the most fierce of the war. Unfortunately, in the smoke, it was hard to observe the fall of shot, and much of the Confederate fire passed over the Union positions.

Finally, the artillery began to run low on ammunition, and Pickett, waiting with his division to make the assault, was warned that unless he advanced now the artillery would have no ammunition left with which to cover him. At this critical juncture it was discovered that no reserve of artillery ammunition was available; Longstreet wanted to stop Pickett until more ammunition could be obtained, but his artillery commander pointed out that such a delay would allow the enemy to recuperate from the bombardment. So Longstreet ordered Pickett to advance, without bothering to inform Lee that the infantry assault was unlikely to be supported by the artillery as Lee expected.

"Pickett's Charge" has, deservedly, gone into history. His division poured from a ravine at the end of the Ridge and were shredded by enfilade fire and frontal howitzers firing case shot. At the same time Hill's six brigades swept down from the Ridge and the two columns converged upon Cemetery Hill. Leaving dead and wounded in their wake, the remnants managed to crown the hill and enter the Union positions, only to be driven off by a strong Union reserve line, and what was left of the assault was eventually driven from the hill and back to its starting point. Lee rode down to meet the survivors, among them Pickett, who cried that his division had been wrecked. "Come, General," said Lee, "this has been my fight and upon my shoulders rests the blame." Roughly two-thirds of Pickett's and Hill's assaulting troops had fallen.

The armies rested in their positions and regarded each other warily; both had suffered about the same amount of casualties – close to 20,000 – and both were aware that in spite of the maulings, each side was still a formidable force. But Lee was principally concerned with conserving his force and beating off counterattacks; his ammunition and food supplies were low, and he was in no position to mount any further offensive. He spent the night working out the orders for the retreat that was inevitable.

**Left:** *Major General George Pickett led a charge of 15,000 Confederate soldiers against the Union lines. A few hundred succeeded while some 9000 fell in the no man's land between Cemetery Ridge and Seminary Ridge.*

**Below:** *A montage of events experienced by Union troops of the 9th Massachusetts Battery at the battle of Gettysburg, beginning with their opening engagement and ending with their departure from the field on July 5.*

# Into the Wilderness

**G**ettysburg was the high point of the Confederacy, and it caused tremors throughout the Union. It was the farthest Confederate intrusion into northern territory, made the Union stand on the defensive in their own parish, caused the alerting of militia far and wide, and, because Meade failed to decisively defeat Lee, gave the latter an aura of invincibility which severely dented northern morale.

The retreat from Gettysburg was carried out in appalling weather, constant rain turning the roads to mud, floods making river crossings perilous, Union raiders destroying bridges, and Meade pressing on Lee's heels. But Meade was dilatory and wasted too much time in careful reconnaissance, so that as the weather abated and the rivers fell, Lee was able to get his army across the Potomac at Falling Waters, southwest of Hagerstown. Meade's attack eventually began, but by that time only Lee's rearguard remained and they beat off the Union advance long enough to allow the whole of Lee's army to get across the rickety bridge.

Once clear of danger the army moved into the Shenandoah Valley to rest and recover from its ordeal, but the rest was a short one since Meade also crossed the Potomac and, east of the mountains, headed toward Richmond. Lee therefore had to march his army east to place himself between Meade and his objective, and by August he had settled in the region of Culpeper, some 40 miles west of Fredericksburg. By this time many southerners had begun to mull over Gettysburg and the surrender of Vicksburg, and were loud in expressing doubts as to the competency of Lee, and questioning reasons for the failure of his campaign. Lee, suffering from sciatica and feeling low, wrote Davis offering his resignation, saying, "I cannot even accomplish what I myself desire. How can I fulfill the expectations of others?"

Davis replied with a friendly letter that said, in effect, that since there was nobody in sight even approaching Lee's caliber, how could Davis hope to find a replacement if Lee resigned? There was no more talk of resignation, and Lee turned himself to the thankless task of trying to keep his army a viable fighting force. Reduced by casualties and illness, desertion and draft evasion, starved of food, clothing and every other necessary supply, the Army of Northern Virginia was no longer such an effective force as it had been at Chancellorsville or even Gettysburg. Indeed, things were so bad that instead of employing cavalry for reconnaissance, they were largely used for foraging.

Davis now produced his maps and organizational charts and began shuffling formations, largely to reinforce the Confederate strength in the West, where Chattanooga, Tennessee, was now under threat. Longstreet's corps, with two extra divisions and extra artillery, went West, more troops were detached to reinforce besieged Charleston, and Pickett's division was split up and scattered throughout North Carolina, leaving Lee with a severely reduced force with which to face Meade, should Meade decide to move.

Lee fell ill again in September, with rheumatic pains that modern analysts have suggested was actually angina. During this time the Union threat to Chattanooga, led by General William S. Rosecrans, was driven off by the combined forces of General Braxton Bragg and General Longstreet, though Bragg neglected to pursue and thus allowed the Union army to fall back in good order. This campaign cured Longstreet of his desire for glory, which was something. Bragg's officers complained, but Bragg was a favorite of Davis, and Davis responded by dispersing the complainers and splitting up Bragg's army, sending Longstreet to conduct a futile siege at Knoxville, Tennessee.

However, a result of all this western maneuvering was that Meade sent two corps to assist Rosecrans in a fresh attack on Chattanooga, and when Lee heard of this he decided to take advantage of Meade's weakened condition and force him out of his threatening positions. He moved around Meade's flank and swung up in the direction of Washington; this had the desired effect of moving Meade,

**Right:** *Lincoln (head bowed at left center) delivering his Gettysburg Address. The significance of this event was not widely recognized at the time. One newspaper reported, "The President also spoke."*

who retired gradually and cautiously northward. Eventually he made a mistake and allowed his rearguard to become vulnerable, and Lee ordered A. P. Hill to attack it.

Hill, careless of planning, attacked far too quickly, with the result that he suffered severe casualties and the Union troops escaped without too much damage. But at least Lee had achieved his aim of getting the Army of the Potomac back on the defensive and closer to Washington. The trouble now was that his supply lines were overstretched and his army too weak to take advantage; he could no longer think realistically of crossing the Potomac or launching any attack, and the dwindling supplies made it vital that he should, instead, fall back to a position in which he could at least be fed. So the army retired to the Rappahannock River area where there was a convenient rail link with Richmond for supplies.

By November Meade was back facing Lee across the Rappahannock, and Lee drew back further, behind the Rapidan. On November 26 Meade sent his army across the Rapidan into the Chancellorsville area, and Lee rapidly deployed two corps to take him in the flank. Meade, however, turned to face Lee, and his two corps then dug themselves into a sound defensive position along Mine Run, a small creek off the Rapidan. Meade made his plans for assault and began an artillery bombardment, but he then had second thoughts about launching an attack into such a well-defended position in broken and thickly wooded country. While he was having these thoughts Jeb Stuart's cavalry found that Meade's right flank was in the air. Lee proposed an outflanking movement, but Meade suddenly realized how vulnerable he was and pulled back across the Rapidan before Lee could move against him. Lee was extremely disappointed; "I am too old to command this army; we should

**Above:** *After Gettysburg, Meade moved with more determination against the Confederate retreat. Skirmishes broke out, including this one at Boonesboro.*

**Overleaf:** *General George Meade (seated at center) with his staff in Culpeper, Virginia, occupied by Union soldiers as Lee withdrew across the Rapidan River.*

never have permitted those people to get away," he said. In freezing weather the two armies fell back to take up winter quarters in Virginia, Meade close to Culpeper, and Lee near Orange County Courthouse. The campaigning season was over for 1863.

By this time President Lincoln had had enough of the ineptitude of his generals and he turned at last to the one Union general who appeared to have more aptitude for fighting than for strutting around Washington in an ornate uniform; he called Ulysses S. Grant from the West and placed him in command of the Union forces. And when Grant got to Washington and saw the awe with which Lee was regarded, he decided that he would have to take personal charge of the fighting in the East. So for the spring of 1864 Lee had a new opponent and, moreover, one of whom he knew very little.

The only thing that appeared to be certain about Grant was that he was not a particularly devious tactician and generally moved in straight lines towards his objective. And since his objective was presumably Richmond, he would be unlikely to perform any wide circling movements – a left flanking march would demand two crossings of the Rappahannock, a right flanking march would take him too far from his supply routes – it seemed that Grant's likeliest course

enabled them to break the Union attack and drive it back; seven Confederate brigades routed a Union corps. By the afternoon, when the Union forces collected their wits, Ewell had dug his three divisions well in and stood on the defensive. Having done that, he ignored the rest of the battle; he neither asked for orders nor sent reports to Lee.

Lee was without reliable information, and was unaware that a wide gap lay between Ewell and A. P. Hill's corps; had he but known it, he could have sliced the Army of the Potomac in half. But without information he merely waited, until a Union patrol burst out of the woods and almost captured him. Lee and his entourage vanished into their own area of woods and escaped harm, but the incident, small as it was,

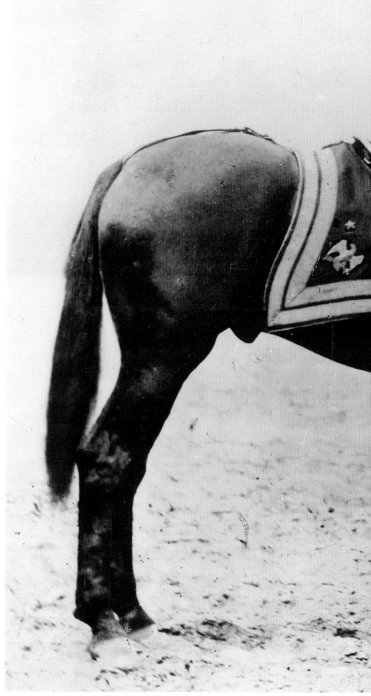

**Above:** *Confederate General A. P. Hill was in danger of being routed from his position in the Wilderness until the timely appearance of Longstreet.*

**Right:** *Lee's formidable new opponent, General Ulysses S. Grant, the newly appointed commander of Union forces.*

was to plunge into the Wilderness, north of Chancellorsville. Once Lee had divined that, he made his plans. The only thing Lee did not know was that Richmond wasn't Grant's objective; Grant was a simple soldier who, with Lincoln, instinctively grasped what many soldiers and most politicians overlooked – that the object of war is to destroy the opposing army, not capture cities. Destroy the enemy and everything else follows. Grant's objective was Lee's army.

Lee reasoned that Grant would move through the roads of the Wilderness; he therefore spread his forces around the area so that they could be moved in any direction to catch Grant in this unfavorable terrain. So secure was he of his plan that he kept it entirely to himself, not telling his commanders what he expected, merely telling them to be ready for orders.

Grant indeed moved exactly as Lee had predicted, but he was screened by strong cavalry forces led by General Philip H. Sheridan, and Jeb Stuart's patrols were unable to get close enough to obtain precise information.

On the morning of May 5 Grant set his army moving into the Wilderness; Lee ordered Ewell to advance until he met the enemy, but not to bring on a general engagement until Longstreet's force arrived in the area. Unfortunately, Ewell ran straight into a major Union advance; the Union force followed Grant's order: "If any opportunity presents itself for pitching into a part of Lee's army, do so without giving time for disposition." The battle was joined.

Initially the Union division overcame the Confederate brigade it had met, but Confederate reinforcements were quick to appear and the thick undergrowth (with which many of them were familiar) gave them an advantage which appears to have given Lee an insight into the way the battle was moving. He now sent a division off to find Ewell's flank, and instructed Heth to try and take a road intersection which appeared to be vulnerable. But the delay had given Grant time to bring up troops; these were flung against Heth as they arrived on the scene, and this lack of cohesion allowed Heth the chance to beat them off piecemeal and set up a defensive position. Lee rapidly called back the division he had sent to find Ewell, ordering them to reinforce Heth, and the battle in Heth's front became, as one contender later said, "a bushwhacking contest," with firing going on in all directions as men dodged in and out of the undergrowth and trees.

**Above:** *A portrait of Confederate General James Longstreet, who arrived with reinforcements to salvage the Wilderness battle of May 6, 1864, for Lee. Longstreet was injured during the battle.*

The day ended in a stalemate as darkness fell, and men rested where they were. During the night Lee considered his options and decided that, once Longstreet's corps arrived with reinforcements, he would carry the battle to Grant. He assumed that, like every previous Union general, Grant would now sit back, lick his wounds, contemplate his losses, and generally stop to make up his mind, during which period Lee would have the chance to counteract. Unfortunately for Lee, Grant was a general who recked nothing of casualties or setbacks; his answer was merely to throw more soldiers in. Consequently, Lee turned down suggestions to concentrate his forces during the night and prepare a defensive line; he was content to let his men rest, sure that Longstreet would arrive during the night to strengthen the line and relieve the most tired troops. But Longstreet had not moved as quickly as he should have, and had not arrived by daybreak.

And while Longstreet was still three miles behind Lee's positions, marching several hours late, Grant struck. The initial Union rush carried them well into the Confederate lines, but they were suddenly confronted with a well-placed battery of artillery which stopped them in their tracks. After the first shock, Union forces began to spread out and outflank the gun position, but this check had been long enough to allow Longstreet to finally reach the field, and without hesitation his divisions flew at the enemy. They were halted and then driven back.

Lee now discovered that the Union flank was exposed, and sent four brigades of fresh troops around to take it in the rear. Using an unfinished railroad cut, the flanking force was able to get around and roll back the Union line in confusion, its alignment totally disrupted by the dense woodland. Longstreet, suddenly seized with inspiration, set about ordering another flanking movement, but was hit by a

**Left:** *An episode in the Wilderness Campaign: Rebel troops capture a part of the burning Union breastworks on Brock Road on May 6.*

**Right:** *Confederate lines awaiting their orders in the Wilderness.*

**Below:** *On May 11, 1864, Jeb Stuart's cavalry confronted Sheridan's at Yellow Tavern, Virginia. During the attack General Stuart was mortally wounded and died the next day.*

stray bullet and severely wounded. Lee took over control of Longstreet's troops, but by the time he had determined who was where and got them organized to make a move, the Union forces had managed to build rough breastworks and form a defensive line. The day ended with the Confederates pressing hard and Grant's army hanging on by its fingernails, but being steadily reinforced with fresh troops.

Grant had suffered 17,000 casualties, Lee less than half that, and most of those were lightly wounded. But in spite of the Union errors, Lee simply did not have the numbers necessary to force a decision. His troops sensed this and during the night were busily digging themselves in and building breastworks, against the Union attack which the next day would undoubtedly bring.

To their surprise, Grant did not attack on the next day; instead he began slipping his forces sideways, moving them southeast towards Spotsylvania, Virginia. His intention was to threaten Lee with an outflanking maneuver, so causing Lee to respond by moving sideways and counterattacking at a point chosen by Grant, who, all the time, would be sliding sideways, threatening Lee's supply routes and getting closer to Richmond.

Lee, however, had foreseen Grant's action; he appreciated that Grant would not go back but would continue to press in one way or another, and Lee considered that the next likely meeting point would be Spotsylvania. And since Grant's move was a looping curve, Lee, moving in a straight line, got there first. When the Union troops arrived at Spotsylvania they found Jeb Stuart's cavalry waiting for them. Gradually the cavalry retired and the Union troops pressed on, only to find the fields thickly sown with Confederate infantry who remained hidden until Grant's advancing force

was within range. After the initial shock the two lines set up barricades, dug trenches, and settled down to hammer each other for two days. Sheridan, chafing at the static action, received permission to take a raiding force south and find Jeb Stuart's cavalry: he set forth with 10,000 horsemen, met Stuart a week later, and in the battle Jeb Stuart was killed by a bullet. Lee wept when he heard the news.

The Confederate line had a prominent salient near its center which Grant decided to chop off; Lee saw that it was vulnerable and had his men prepare a fall-back position. Grant feinted, drew Lee's artillery off to a flank, then struck the salient on three sides in darkness. The subsequent battle for the "Bloody Angle" was probably the most bitter and expensive single fight of the Civil War, the dead piling up on both sides. But the Confederates fell back to their breastworks in good order and continued to dispute the Angle, and Grant hammered in vain. So he decided to slip to his left once more.

This time they met across the North Anna River, and Lee, in a brilliant tactical stroke, when threatened with being flanked on both sides by Grant, formed his army into a spearhead resting on the river and so split the Army of the Potomac as to render it incapable of action against him. Grant, frustrated, slipped sideways yet again. By this time Lee was sick once more, this time with an intestinal complaint, and incapable of taking the field, so that he tended to settle for defensive action rather than initiate offensive moves which he could not personally control nor trust to his subordinates. Although he could foresee with astonishing accuracy the courses that Grant would take, he had neither the personal strength nor the reliable commanders to take advantage of his prescience.

# The Road to Appomattox

Lee and Grant came to grips again at Cold Harbor, a few miles northeast of Richmond, and Grant was determined to settle with Lee once and for all; if he failed, Lee could retire into the formidable fortifications of Richmond, leaving Grant the prospect of a long and difficult siege. On June 1, 1864 the Union army threw itself at Lee's defenses. There was no tactical cleverness or subtle maneuvering – a straightforward, all-out frontal assault was the only option open to Grant. It was so obvious that most of the Union troops spent the previous night stitching name tags on their coats so that their bodies could be identified.

The attack failed, at enormous cost, some 10,000 Union men falling in the fruitless assault. Even Grant, hard fighter as he might be, could scarcely afford losses on that scale and he forebore to mount a second assault. The two armies lay behind their breastworks, and after nine days Grant slipped away in the night. But this time his move was totally out of character – or, at least, out of the character that Lee

**Right:** *In July 1864, Lee sent a Confederate force under General Jubal Early toward Washington in an attempt to draw some of Grant's army away from Lee. Early attacked from the north, reached Fort Stevens, within five miles of the city, but retired after only two days, having seriously threatened the Capital.*

**Above:** *Confederate defenders of Petersburg practice with their weapons. Grant put both Petersburg and Richmond under a seige that lasted from the summer of 1864 to April 2, 1865, when Grant ordered the Army of the Potomac to take the Petersburg trenches.*

was now accustomed to reading. Instead of another simple sideslip, Grant marched, bridged, marched again and suddenly appeared to the south outside Petersburg, having looped around Richmond, threatening to cut the Confederate supply lines and take the city.

Lee's cavalry was off chasing Sheridan in the west, and thus Lee was blind; until he had some reliable information he preferred to sit tight. With one-tenth of the energy displayed at Cold Harbor, Grant's army could have walked into Petersburg, but the leading commander was tremulous and fearful of casualties. He spent hours over careful reconnaissance, and delayed longer by calling up artillery which was not readily available. The Confederate defenses consisted of a scattering of troops augmented by old men and boys rounded up and thrust into the trenches in desperation; a corporal's guard could have walked over them. But when the Union lines eventually advanced they took the first line of Confederate trenches and then stopped, waiting for reinforcements before moving further.

When morning came it was the Confederate lines that were reinforced; Lee had finally discovered what Grant had done and had rushed troops down the railroad to Petersburg. Moreover, when the Union troops finally did attack, it

was without the fire that had previously distinguished them. They were repulsed, and Grant drew up 35 miles of siege works around both Petersburg and Richmond.

Lee now had the audacity to pull Jubal Early and 20,000 men out of the line and send him off on a raid to Washington which, had Early been more enterprising, might have had significant results. His force looped up through the Valley and descended upon Washington from the north, reaching as far as Fort Stevens, one of the many forts surrounding Washington. Here he demonstrated, with sufficient effect to bring Lincoln himself to the fort and thus become the only U.S. President to come under fire while in office. But after two days of desultory shooting, Early retired, unpursued, having missed a great opportunity, for Washington was poorly manned and the capital was in confusion at the Confederate threat.

The troops within and without Richmond and Petersburg settled down to the routine of a siege; though in fact, it wasn't really a siege since the Confederates still had communication and supply routes in and out of their cities. Nevertheless it became a boring existence for both sides, livened occasionally by some sortie or other surprise. Perhaps the greatest of these was the Union attempt to mine beneath a Confederate position; men labored day and night for weeks to dig a 500-foot tunnel, laid 8000 pounds of powder, then fired it. The Confederate position vanished and in its place was a massive crater. Like almost every effort of this kind, its tactical surprise was nullified by the astonishment of the assaulting troops, who simply stood and gazed at the amazing sight or milled round in the crater

**Right:** *Map of the Federal advance on the Confederate strongholds of Richmond and Petersburg.*

**Far right:** *The final Union assault on Petersburg. That same day, April 2, Richmond was evacuated.*

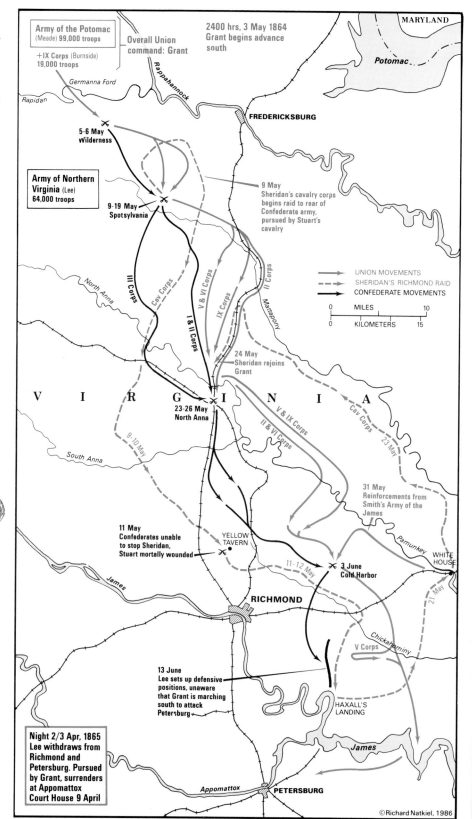

Army of the Potomac (Meade) 99,000 troops

Overall Union command: Grant

+IX Corps (Burnside) 19,000 troops

Germanna Ford

Rapidan

Rappahannock

2400 hrs, 3 May 1864 Grant begins advance south

MARYLAND

Potomac

FREDERICKSBURG

5-6 May Wilderness

Army of Northern Virginia (Lee) 64,000 troops

9-19 May Spotsylvania

9 May Sheridan's cavalry corps begins raid to rear of Confederate army, pursued by Stuart's cavalry

North Anna

III Corps

Cav Corps

V & VI Corps

I & II Corps

IX Corps

II Corps

Mattapony

UNION MOVEMENTS
SHERIDAN'S RICHMOND RAID
CONFEDERATE MOVEMENTS

0 MILES 10
0 KILOMETERS 15

24 May Sheridan rejoins Grant

V I R G I N I A

23-26 May North Anna

V & IX Corps

II & VI Corps

Cav Corps

23 May

9-10 May

South Anna

31 May Reinforcements from Smith's Army of the James

Pamunkey

WHITE HOUSE

11 May Confederates unable to stop Sheridan, Stuart mortally wounded

YELLOW TAVERN

11-12 May

3 June Cold Harbor

21 May

James

RICHMOND

Chickahominy

V Corps

13 June Lee sets up defensive positions, unaware that Grant is marching south to attack Petersburg

HAXALL'S LANDING

James

Night 2/3 Apr, 1865 Lee withdraws from Richmond and Petersburg. Pursued by Grant, surrenders at Appomattox Court House 9 April

Appomattox

PETERSBURG

©Richard Natkiel, 1986

**Above:** *An artist's sketch of Lee riding his faithful horse, Traveller.*

trying to climb out, giving sufficient time for the defenders to rush troops up to the lip of the crater from which they shot into the mob beneath. The Battle of the Crater cost Grant another 4000 casualties.

The North held an election, with McClellan running against Lincoln and losing; Christmas came and went; and still the siege wore on. Finally, in February 1865 Grant moved, stretching out his left flank around Petersburg to cut the Confederate supply line. There were tentative suggestions for a meeting between Lee and Grant to try and arrange some peaceful solution, but both Lincoln and Davis vetoed the idea. But by now Lee's force had dwindled to 35,000 while Grant had something like 175,000 facing him, and Lee realized that things were unlikely to get better.

Davis finally agreed that the loss of Richmond could be borne provided Lee was able to continue the fight elsewhere, and at the end of March Lee sprang an attack on the Union Fort Stedman opposite Petersburg. This was a success, the Fort was taken and thousands of Confederate troops spread out around it, splitting the Army of the Potomac in two. Lee reasoned that Grant might now pull back his left wing to reinforce the breach, leaving the way open for Lee to disengage and rush southwards to join General Joseph E. Johnston in North Carolina, there to continue the war. But Grant had sufficient reserves of artillery and infantry to drive in the Confederate assault, retake his fort and resume the status quo without moving his left, and Lee's chance evaporated.

Four days later Grant began his spring campaign by a massive assault from his left wing. With Sheridan and 10,000 cavalry in the vanguard, the Confederate positions were rolled up with the loss of 5000 prisoners, and the route south was firmly closed. Lee had only one option; to abandon Richmond and move westward. He advised Davis "that all preparations be made for leaving Richmond tonight," to which Davis replied that the Government would not have time to save all their records and files. Lee is reputed to have torn up this reply and flung it into the mud. Throughout the night of April 2 the Confederate troops abandoned their lines and marched through Richmond and across the James River. Demolition of warehouses, stores and government equipment was begun, and the sparks and flames spread to houses and shops so that a third of Richmond was eventually burned down. The Union army marched in, the Union flag was raised over the Confederate capital, and the North went mad with joy.

Before leaving Richmond Lee had carefully ordered trainloads of supplies to be dispatched from the South to await his arrival at Amelia Courthouse, about 40 miles away. When his 30,000 strong army arrived there they found ammunition, but no food; some administrative blunder had routed the ration trains to Lynchburg, where they were now in Union hands. There was no alternative to foraging among the local community, which held out little promise for an army of that size. Meanwhile Sheridan had moved ahead and was reporting to Grant that he had now settled astride Lee's only route out of Amelia Courthouse. Grant busied himself with sending out troops to cover every possible avenue of movement; whatever direction Lee took, there would be Union troops blocking his route.

Throughout the next day Sheridan's fast-moving cavalry pounced on the Confederate column as it lurched, starving and sleepless, through the countryside. At Sayler's Creek General Ewell, Lee's son Custis and 3000 men were captured. Men surrendered, others simply drifted away into the

**Left:** *Sketch by Civil War artist A. R. Waud of Confederate officers crossing the James River by pontoon bridge as they come into Richmond to give themselves up.*

**Above:** *Union soldiers look at the ruins of Richmond after it was abandoned by its defenders. It would be years before the city would regain its prewar prosperity.*

that portion of the C. S. Army known as the Army of Northern Virginia." And under the protection of a white flag, this message was sent off through the lines.

Now began a succession of messages; Lee replied that while he was not so despondent of his position as was Grant, nevertheless "I reciprocate your desire to avoid the useless effusion of blood" and what terms was Grant thinking of offering? Grant, after all, was the man who coined the phrase "unconditional surrender" and Lee wanted to find out just what he had in mind. Grant's reply was reassuring; the only condition he insisted upon was that those who laid down their arms would promise not to take them up again. And while these messages passed to and fro, the Confederate column kept up its slow struggle westward, the men foraging in the fields for anything they could find to sustain them.

Grant's last message reached Lee in the morning, just as several of his staff officers were suggesting that the only reasonable course must be surrender, before the troops starved to death. Lee replied to Grant that "I did not intend to propose the surrender . . . but to ask the terms of your proposition. To be frank, I do not think the emergency has arisen to call for the surrender of this army." However, he went on, he would be happy to meet Grant and discuss how peace could be restored.

Grant received this message in the early hours of April 9,

woods, many collapsed and waited for the pursuing Union troops to capture them. Sheridan telegraphed to Grant "If the thing is pressed, I think Lee will surrender," to which Lincoln replied, when informed of the message, "Let the thing be pressed."

On the evening of April 7, Grant wrote a letter to Lee: "The results of the last week must convince you of the hopelessness of further resistance on the part of the Army of Northern Virginia in this struggle. I feel that it is so, and regard it as my duty to shift from myself the responsibility of any further effusion of blood, by asking of you the surrender of

**Left:** *On April 1 Union General Sheridan's troops destroyed General Pickett's force at Five Forks, capturing 6000 Rebels. The loss forced Lee to pull out of Petersburg the next night.*

**Left below:** *The ruins of General Lee's headquarters at Petersburg, in a drawing by A. R. Waud.*

**Right:** *A drawing made after Appomattox of the respected general-in-chief of the Army of the Confederacy.*

Palm Sunday. His reply was to the effect that he had no remit to discuss peace terms, merely surrender, and that the proposed meeting would therefore be pointless.

Early in the morning, Confederate infantry under General John B. Gordon made a last desperate attack against Union cavalry which was pressing too close. The cavalry was driven back, but Union infantry were called up. Gordon sent a message to Lee, "I have fought my corps to a frazzle and I fear I can do nothing unless I am heavily supported by Longstreet's corps." But Longstreet was trying to hold off another wing of the Union army; the Confederates were completely surrounded by far superior numbers. And when this was apparent to Lee, he reached his final conclusion:

"There is nothing left for me but to go and see General Grant, and I would rather die a thousand deaths." He sent off a message to be carried through the lines immediately: "I received your note of this morning with reference to the surrender of this army. I now request an interview in accordance with that purpose." The word gradually spread across the lines and the firing slowly died away.

Lee dressed himself in his best uniform. "I have probably to be Grant's prisoner and thought I had better make my best appearance," he explained to his staff. An aide from General Grant arrived, to arrange the meeting place, and shortly after he had left, Lee mounted his horse and headed for Appomattox Court House.

# From Hero to Myth

**G**rant was not a vindictive man – professional soldiers rarely are – and in spite of his varied career, Grant was a professional soldier. Lee was relieved to discover, when he finally sat down opposite Grant at Appomattox Court House, that the terms Grant was offering were relatively simple: that the officers and men surrender to be paroled and disqualified from taking up arms until properly exchanged, and that all arms, ammunition and supplies be delivered up. The only caveat Lee entered was to point out that in the Confederate army the cavalry and mounted artillerymen owned their own horses; could they not retain them so as to put them to use when they returned home to their farms? Grant agreed to this condition, and Lee replied that "This will have the best possible effect upon the men. It will be very gratifying and will do much toward conciliating our people."

Lee then pointed out that he had over a thousand Union prisoners, that he would like to hand back since he had no means of feeding them. The hint was taken, and Grant arranged for 25,000 rations to be delivered to the Confederates. He tactfully omitted to say that they were, in fact, the contents of the misdirected Confederate supply trains he had captured when they reached Appomattox station.

And with that the war, for Lee and his men, was over. He left Grant and rode back into his own lines where, during his meeting, word had spread and men had crowded to the road to see what was happening. Lee rode back through a crowd of his soldiers; the usual cheering broke out but rapidly died down when the men saw the grim expression on his face. Finally, one man asked, "General, are we surrendered?" Lee stopped, removed his hat, looked at his men, and in a voice thick with emotion, replied, "Men, we

**Right:** *General Lee and his staff ride away from the McLean House after the surrender at Appomattox Court House, Virginia.*

have fought the war together, and I have done the best I could for you. You will all be paroled and go to your homes. Goodbye." And he resumed his progress through the crowd.

According to Lee's final report to Jefferson Davis, which he wrote on April 11, he had 7892 organized infantry with arms present for duty when he surrendered. Over the course of the next few days, however, thousands of stragglers and disorganized and unarmed men drifted in, especially when the word got around that food had arrived. The terms of the surrrender were extended to a 20-mile radius around Appomattox, and eventually some 28,231 officers and men were listed on the parole records. In spite of this, Davis announced that the war would continue, though without an organized army it is hard to see how he thought he could do so.

On April 12 came the formal surrender, when the Army of Northern Virginia formed up under arms for the last time, marched to a designated spot, and piled their arms, hung their cartridge pouches on the rifles, draped their colors across them and then filed off under the eyes of ranks of silent Union troops. The marching groups returned to their starting point to be finally dismissed, then walked away from the scene of their final military act as civilians on their way home to pick up their interrupted lives once more. Among them was Lee, riding his horse and accompanied by a few of his headquarters staff, heading for Richmond and a reunion with his wife and family.

On April 15, the word spread throughout Richmond that General Lee was returning, and by the time he reached the James River crowds were lining the streets. There was no cheering; men removed their hats as he passed, and witnesses spoke of a "deep, loving murmur" which arose from the crowd. Lee doffed his own hat and bowed his head as he rode silently by, until he arrived at his house, dismounted, entered, and the door closed behind him.

**Above:** *Federal soldiers at the east front of Arlington Mansion on June 28, 1864. Lee's home until acquired by the Federal government in a tax sale in January, it was made headquarters of the Arlington National Cemetery later in the year.*

**Below:** *Thomas Nast, noted cartoonist and illustrator on the staff of* Harper's Weekly, *drew this version of the surrender of General Robert E. Lee. It surmounted a prayer to "Honor the illustrious dead."*

After four years of arduous service, marked by unsurpassed courage and fortitude, the Army of Northern Virginia has been compelled to yield to overwhelming numbers and resources. I need not tell the brave survivors of so many hard-fought battles, who have remained steadfast to the last, that I have consented to this result from no distrust of them; but feeling that valor and devotion could accomplish nothing that would compensate for the loss that must have attended a continuance of the contest, I determined to avoid the useless sacrifice of those whose past services have endeared them to their countrymen. By the terms of agreement officers and men can return to their homes and remain until exchanged. You will take with you the satisfaction that proceeds from the consciousness of duty faithfully performed, and I earnestly pray that a merciful God will extend to you His blessing and protection. With an increasing admiration of your constancy and devotion to your country and a grateful remembrance of your kind and generous consideration of myself, I bid you all an affectionate farewell.

APRIL 10th, 1865.

STRATFORD HOUSE, VIRGINIA, BIRTHPLACE OF LEE.

LEE CHAPEL, VIRGINIA, BENEATH WHICH THE GENERAL WAS BURIED.

**Left:** *An illustrated version of Robert E. Lee's farewell address, with insets showing his birthplace and the place where he is buried.*

**Right:** *Soldiers weep as the Confederate battle flag is furled for the last time.*

Staying rigidly within the limits imposed by his parole, Lee remained indoors for several days, apparently spending most of the time in bed, catching up on his rest and recuperating from the strain of the final campaign. There was a constantly changing group of well-wishers outside his door waiting for a glimpse of their general, but few saw him. A stream of callers came but most were skillfully fended off by Fitzhugh, Lee's nephew. One significant caller was Mathew Brady, the celebrated photographer who, after several rebuffs, was finally able to photograph Lee in the uniform he had worn at Appomattox. Occasionally Lee

would walk out in the evening, and in June he went into the countryside to stay with Thomas Carter, a relative.

He arrived back in Richmond to hear that he had been indicted for treason; he wrote to Grant, pointing out that the terms of the surrender guaranteed freedom from such charges and enclosed an application for amnesty addressed to President Johnson. Although Johnson, a vindictive man, was unwilling to relinquish the prospect of trying both Lee and Davis for their lives, Grant managed to quash the indictment and nothing more was heard of it.

Lee's principal concern at this time was the very basic

one of how to earn a living. He was 58 years of age, a soldier without an army and with no professional qualifications. He had been offered one or two sinecures in which he was expected to give his name to various ventures in return for directorships, but he turned these down; in his view there was something not quite honest about cashing in on his name.

In Lexington, Virginia, at the same time a small college was casting about for a new president. Washington College was not a very large institution, with but four professors and a handful of students, situated as it was in a remote area with poor communications. In the course of a meeting of trustees, Lee's name was brought up, and from there it was a short step to a formal motion that he be approached. Having made the minute in the records, the trustees were slightly appalled at their temerity, but decided to go ahead; the worst that could happen would be that Lee would merely say no. And in order to put the proposal to Lee one of the trustees borrowed a suit and the fare and set off for Richmond.

Lee's friends and relatives were shocked at the idea; if Lee was to run a university, there were plenty of bigger and better ones that would be happy to have him. Lee, on the other hand, saw beyond the mere title and into the heart of the matter; in his view, this gave an opportunity to begin the rebuilding of the South by the education of its youth. He accepted the post, set off for Lexington, and, once there, found that as well as being president of the college he was also dean, bursar, registrar, head gardener and general factotum. His salary was $125 a month and he had a single secretary to help him. Nevertheless, he set to with a will, and busied himself in organizing the college and writing to influential men to beg for donations.

Once the president's house was ready, Lee's wife joined him, together with her daughters. Lee's sons were busy attempting to salvage the family estates, though Arlington had gone forever, forfeited for nonpayment of taxes during the war when the Union authorities insisted that delinquent taxpayers had to make payment in person, and it was by this time surrounded by a military cemetery – as it still is.

As college president Lee led by example; he avoided a rigorous curriculum and formal discipline, preferring to allow students some liberty – for, after all, many had served as soldiers and a return to the discipline of the schoolroom would have been ridiculous – and to allow the affairs of the college to be gently debated by the faculty rather than be imposed by decree. He avoided all reference to the war, never discussed it, read nothing of the prolific memoirs and accounts produced by his contemporaries, but spent his afternoons riding Traveller, the horse who had carried him through the war. Lexington was well away from the center of things, and few of Lee's old acquaintances passed that way; when they did, their inevitable reaction was to observe that Lee had aged and the fire had gone out of him.

Nevertheless, under Lee's guidance Washington College prospered. The student body increased to 400, the curriculum was widened, new buildings were gradually added, and as the fame of the college spread, so students came from all over the United States. Plans were laid for courses in business studies, for founding of a school of agriculture and for a model farm to be added to the campus, but as the months went by Lee's physical condition began to deteriorate. He was treated for rheumatism, lumbago and other complaints, but the plain fact was that his heart was wearing out.

In the spring of 1869 he was persuaded to visit Baltimore, in an endeavor to raise money for a railroad project. Crowds turned out in the streets to cheer his passing. From Baltimore he went to Washington, invited there by General, now President, Grant; after a formal welcome, the two old antagonists sat down alone for a short conversation (to which neither ever referred in any detail) and Lee left Washington for the last time.

**Right:** *General Robert E. Lee mounted on his famous mare Traveller. The horse became a legend to the soldiers of the Confederate Army for her strength and beauty.*

**Below:** *The funeral of Robert E. Lee, October 1870, at Lee Chapel, where he is buried, on the campus of Washington and Lee University.*

Returned from Washington, Lee began to doubt his ability to continue. His former erect bearing had gone, every movement was painful, and he felt that a fitter man should be guiding the college. His talk of resignation was dismissed, and the faculty, early in 1870, suggested that he should go south for a holiday to regain his health. He set off with his daughter Agnes in March, and what began as a family holiday rapidly turned into a progression. Once the news spread throughout the South that General Lee was coming, crowds turned out in every town and village on his route, bands greeted his train at every station, dignitaries vied to give speeches, Confederate veterans paraded, delegations of officers called upon him. "I do not think that travelling in this way procures me much quiet or repose," he wrote in a letter to his wife. Whatever precautions he took to try and move unnoticed, he was unsuccessful, and his every move was dogged by admiring throngs. Eventually he tired of the commotion and made his weary way back to Lexington.

The summer of 1870 was unusually hot, and Lee tired easily; he could no longer ride Traveller. In the fall the students assembled, classes began and the weather broke. On September 28 it rained, and Lee had to attend a church vestrymen's meeting, where he sat in a cold room in his wet clothes listening to interminable discussion about the minister's wages. In the end, to cut short what looked like going on all night, he promised $55 to make up the necessary sum, then returned home. He entered his house, stood silent, then collapsed into a chair; his wife sent for a doctor.

The doctors conferred and put him to bed. For two days he slept most of the time, and after that he seemed to improve and began taking a little food. But he appeared to have been under few illusions; when offered medicine by one of his daughters, he refused, saying, "It is of no use."

For two weeks he stayed in bed, and during that time the weather turned foul, with heavy rain and, most remarkable for that latitude, an aurora in the northern sky which many took to be an omen. On October 10 Lee's pulse and breathing speeded up and he suffered shivering spells. On the following day his mind wandered off into the past and he occasionally called out some long-forgotten name. "Tell Hill he must come up!" he cried. His wife sat holding his hand through the night, until just after nine o'clock in the morning of October 12, 1870, Lee roused himself. "Strike the tent!" he cried, and then fell back in his final rest.

What was it about Lee that turned him from a soldier into

**Right:** *Mary Randolph Custis Lee, a great granddaughter of Martha Washington and the wife of Robert E. Lee for 40 years.*

a nation's symbol? For today the name of Lee is still revered in a manner to which few generals and fewer leaders attain. In a word, he was a gentleman, and this no more so than in those few years after the war when gentleness was being swamped by immigration and the bustle of rebuilding a nation. Not for Lee the vainglorious memoirs, the accolades, the honorary dignities, the purses, the estates affected by his contemporaries. He finished his life the same way that he had lived it, quietly, seeking to serve rather than to be served. And it is this quiet dignity and selflessness that runs like a thread throughout his life and which endeared him to everyone. Not only did he lead his native state in war, he also did his best to lead it in the way it should go in peace, and for that he deserves honor.

Nevertheless, it has to be said that gentleness is not the best metal from which to forge a victorious general, and it is to Lee's credit that he achieved the military results he did in spite of his natural tendencies and in spite of the difficulties placed in his way. There is little doubt that had Jefferson Davis appointed Lee as overall commander on the day war was declared, the South might well have survived independently. If war had to be, then the victory of the North was inevitable; this is a simple economic and strategic fact which cannot be argued. The manpower and industrial potential of the North made its eventual victory assured. But under Lee the South, in the early days of the war, would undoubtedly have been able to deliver some severe setbacks to the emerging Union army which, who knows, might have been sufficient to make the politicians think twice and settle for things as they were. It is an interesting speculation.

"If Lee had not been fettered by Davis" is one ground for speculation. The second is "If Lee had not been hampered

**Above:** *The memorial to the Confederate Army at Stone Mountain, Georgia. Begun in 1923 by American sculptor Gutzon Borglum and completed in 1970 (the actual work took only 11 years), it features figures of Lee, Jefferson Davis and Stonewall Jackson.*

**Right:** *The distinguished commander in the uniform of a Confederate colonel, the dress he preferred despite his senior rank.*

by ineffective and willful subordinates." Time and again during his campaigns, dereliction of duty by some subordinate either brought the South far too close to disaster or prevented the South from reaping the victory that Lee's planning ought to have secured. Lee's greatest fault as a general lay in his reluctance to give specific and firm orders; he preferred to suggest and guide rather than to deliver edicts. And with subordinates of the caliber of Longstreet and others, this was fatal. Officers who would have balked at deliberately disobeying a firm order saw no shame in equally deliberately dismissing a suggestion or turning a blind eye to a proposal which, from Lee, was tantamount to an order. Holding together a collection of military prima donnas is no job for a gentleman, and senior generals frequently are prima donnas, otherwise they would not be senior generals. It therefore demands a firm hand as well as a clear head to be a commander-in-chief. It was Lee's strength and weakness that he was no tyrant, but a gentleman. And when the tyrants have been forgotten, Lee will still be remembered for that.

# Index